The Moses Gap

The Moses Gap

Alice I. Henry

Published by Salt Water Media
29 Broad Street, Suite 104
Berlin, MD 21811
www.saltwatermedia.com

Salt Water
MEDIA

The cover image is "The Finding of Moses" by Sir Lawrence
Alma-Tadema and is in the public domain.

Interior images are courtesy of the author
and/or in the public domain

"To God be the glory, great things He has done..."
Hymn by Lou Fellingham

For my family—for my husband, who has heard about this book, as a work in progress, for forty-three years—thank you for your great support. The time has finally come for the book to be "really" finished! For Guy—now you know it all, before anyone else. For Ollie and Jenny—I am so proud of both of you. For my grandchildren—Caitlin, Emma, Liam, and Naomi—and for my great-granddaughter, Ivy.

Contents

Introduction

From a young age, I have always been intrigued by ancient Egypt. When studying early civilizations in school, I eagerly anticipated learning about ancient Egyptian history. Many years later, whenever I either studied the Bible myself or led others in Bible studies, the Book of Exodus always captured my interest. As I absorbed its contents, my desire to know all about the historical Moses and the Hebrews in Egypt intensified over time.

Never having traveled to Egypt, the Land of the Pharaohs, I became fascinated with books written about that land by those who had made huge discoveries in the late 19th and early 20th centuries. I began to wonder how the text of the Bible and the facts relayed in Egyptian history might connect with, support, and even confirm each other.

To my dismay, I couldn't find the events that were written about in Exodus in any of the historical books or documents about Ancient Egypt. Thus, in the early 1980s, I became an "armchair Egyptologist" while embarking on my expedition through the pages of available

archaeological and historical accounts authored by famous and lesser-known Egyptologists who had actually
been there. Through the eyes of these pioneers, I began
to see what sort of people the ancient Egyptians had been
and learn how their culture and beliefs had been shaped
by their particular geography. Then I began to discover
the connection I had been seeking—that connection
between Egypt's historical records and the events mentioned in the Bible, namely in Exodus.

As I continued my research, it became clearer and
clearer that this connection had never been written about
in any of the books, documents, discussions, documenta-
ries, and other sources that provided information regarding Ancient Egypt. This is why I wanted to write a book—
needed to write a book—about the things I had found. I
envisioned the reader taking an imaginary journey with
me into the world of Ancient Egypt, specifically during
the period from the end of the XVIII Dynasty (1295 B.C.)
to the beginning of the XIX Dynasty (1295-1187 B.C.).

Although my biblical experience, research, quotes,
and references are from the Christian Bible, other religions share the story of Moses. He is the most important
prophet in Judaism; he is also an important prophet in
Islam, the Bahá'í Faith, and other religions claiming that
their people are descendants of Abraham.

There may be people reading what I've written who
may remain skeptical, who won't be convinced—but that

is not my purpose. I just want to share what I have learned and, hopefully, stir enough of an interest that might lead readers to explore the possibilities for themselves.

Please join me. Pick a comfortable armchair and have an imaginary cup of tea—or coffee, if you prefer—as we set off on our journey.

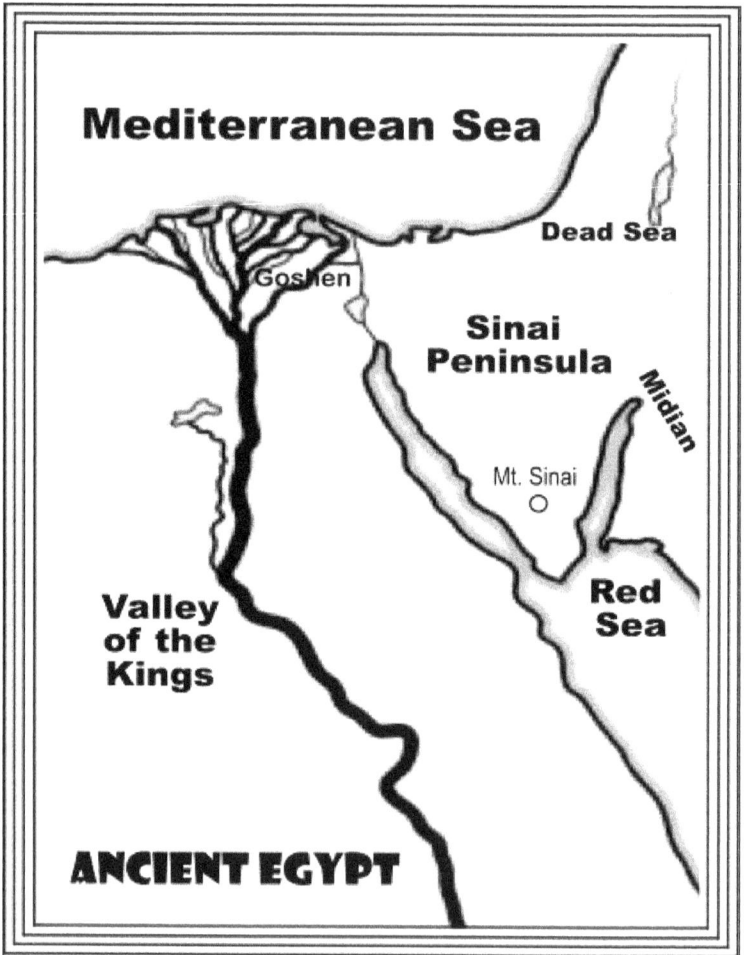

Map of Ancient Egypt
Image courtesy of the author

Preface

C an you imagine the excitement that must have followed the discovery of the Rosetta Stone, in 1799, as soon as it became evident that Egyptian hieroglyphics could finally be deciphered? The stone was inscribed in 196 B.C. with the same message written in Egyptian hieroglyphic and Egyptian demotic characters, as well as in Greek. By comparing the first two to the latter, a key that unlocked the mysteries of this very old culture was found—one that has had an enormous effect on subsequent civilizations.

For many years, there have been conflicts between the Egyptian Museum in Cairo, the British Museum in London, and the Metropolitan Museum in New York City, and, to a lesser degree, among others who house ancient Egyptian treasures. Along with other Egyptian artifacts, the Rosetta Stone has been claimed by and displayed in the British Museum since its discovery. I consider myself fortunate to have been able to see the actual Rosetta Stone at the British Museum. Had it been in Egypt at the time, I might never have enjoyed viewing this treasure.

Not only can ancient Egyptian artifacts be found in

several countries ... ancient Egyptian influence can also be seen in almost every part of the world. Some influences are subtly intertwined in mankind's way of life and beliefs. Others are more obviously displayed: consider the pyramid and eye on our own dollar bill. Perhaps the reason for such a tremendous influence left by an ancient civilization might be that, at its zenith, over three thousand years ago, it was amazingly advanced in many areas including art, literature, medicine, and architecture. Another reason might be the fact that, because it was shrouded with a sense of mystery, superstition, and magic, its eventual utter decline left many of us with curious awe.

Most of us are consciously unaware of the extent of the impact that Egypt has had across the globe, from its earliest days to the present. We find an example of such influence in our own legal system, where the personification of "Justice" holding scales is the counterpart of Mayet, the Egyptian goddess of order and all that is right and just. She always presided at the ceremony in which the heart of a dead person was weighed against his deeds, both good and bad. This image came to us indirectly, as the Greek and Roman empires both adopted and adapted Egyptian customs, religion, and philosophy and handed them down to posterity.

At one time or another, every one of us has admired the beauty, skill, and creativity demonstrated in Egyptian art, architecture, and literature. What great city in the world has not proudly displayed an obelisk, or has not housed authentic Egyptian treasures in its museums? There has always been controversy about how these treasures were obtained and claimed by different countries. In more recent times, Egypt has been actively seeking to repatriate many of these artifacts and objects of historical and cultural significance. The repatriation of various items discovered in Egypt by British, French, and German Egyptologists has been a source of contention for many years. Of course, the Egyptians are within their rights in reclaiming what should be theirs—who could argue with that? However, this is not a matter for me to speculate.

With great curiosity, many of us prod and probe history to search out the enigmas of a people whose civilization thrived for at least three thousand years. We wonder what they were like and how they could have managed such greatness for so long.

Egyptologists have covered most aspects of Ancient Egypt. They have recorded these for us in books about Egyptian history, mythology, customs, family life, and art among many other subjects. This has been made possible by the fact that a wealth of archaeological data exists, preserved beautifully by the dry climate and the protective layers of sand that covered them for thousands of years. Many treasures, manuscripts, paintings, and carvings have been left intact for avid Egyptologists to discover.

Through these sources, we can learn much about what Egyptians were like. From the poorest peasant's humble abode to the incredibly luxurious palaces, Egyptologists tell us that Egyptians lived in harmony with one another and in contentment with their way of life. Their mythology, so complex and varied—even at times contradictory—was unanimously accepted by all Egyptians. They were hedonists, believing their individual gods to be the true and right ones for themselves, yet accepting the gods of other Egyptian cities, and even other countries, to be just as true and right for the people in those distinct areas.

They were a peaceful people, isolated and surrounded by the protective arms of their natural boundaries—on the west, the desert; on the north, the Mediterranean Sea; on the east, the Nile River. Thus nestled, their character was shaped in such a way that, for a long time, they had no need to defend their land from foreign invasion or to go outside their borders to conquer other lands. They were very content within their own country, where all their needs were met.

Information about almost any Egyptian topic can be well-documented by archaeological finds. From these, we can learn intimate details of family life: We learn about the foods they ate; the clothes they wore; how they treated each other; how they behaved in the home, in the palace, and in the priesthood. We can number and even name some of the wives and children of specific pharaohs. Yet, with all the details available, there is one subject about which nothing can be found. It is the topic mentioned in the Bible about Moses and the Hebrew slaves living in Egypt. It is to this specific subject that the remainder of this book will turn its attention.

Our focus will be to try to fill the "Moses gap" that exists between the Bible and the historical records, attempting to prove that Moses was a historical figure who left his indelible footprints on the soil of history's place and time. We will also search for evidence of the people he led—the Hebrews—and the events that surrounded them, showing them all to be recognizably real.

As we set out on our journey, questions may arise: "Could the Bible be wrong?" or "Did a man called Moses really exist?" and "Was he actually groomed in the palace to be the next pharaoh of Egypt, as the Bible states?" We might also ask, "What about the ten plagues and the Exodus?" "Did over six hundred thousand Hebrew male slaves, besides women and children, leave Egypt on foot in one day?" "Were these documented historical events or were they biblical fantasy?" We might even wonder: "Did one of the pharaohs, one of the kings of Egypt who led his army in pursuit of the Hebrews, possibly drown in the Red Sea when the parted waters returned to their natural level?" These are not rhetorical questions. Our curiosity unleashed might lead us to ask: "How did the Hebrews become slaves in Egypt?" "Which king ordered that all male Hebrew babies be put to death?" "If Moses was a historical figure, who was the princess referred to as 'Pharaoh's daughter,' who saved his life?"and "Which king was her father?"

It is important to note that there will appear to be discrepancies in the spelling of Egyptian names throughout this book. The reason: translators differ in their choice of inserted vowels since no vowels existed in the Egyptian language. In addition, the tendency seems to be to write the names phonetically. Thus, at times the name of Haremhab may be written as Horemheb; Akhenaten may be seen as Ikhnaton; Seti as Sethos, and so on. When quoting a particular source, a name will be spelled the way it was written in that source. It may seem that these variations in spelling will be confusing. However, once the reader is aware of the reason for these spelling variations, the understanding of the passage will not be affected. We have no way of knowing how ancient Egyptians pronounced the names; if we get stuck and don't know what a particular name might be, we could try to omit the vowels and sound out the consonants phonetically. I invite you to try this out now with the names mentioned in this paragraph.

At times, I might choose one spelling over another as simply a personal choice— because it might appeal to me in a particular instance. But I assure you that you will always be able to identify the person to whom I refer.

One other point I would like to make: at times, it may seem as if I'm being too repetitious. I probably am...but with good reason: by repeating certain facts, my hope is that you will be more likely to remember them as you continue to read.

Are you ready to embark with me on a journey of exploration in search of answers to some of the questions I've mentioned? By sifting through the dry Egyptian sands of history and time, let us see if we might uncover some clues that could make our search an exciting and successful one.

Chapter I

THE HEBREWS IN EGYPT

The Bible tells us that an enormous Hebrew population lived in Egypt for over four hundred years. It also tells us that, at the end of that period, a man named Moses led them out of Egypt under circumstances that should have been historically recorded for posterity. However, there are no Egyptian historical records that might support such information. Not only are we told by the Bible that these people lived in Egypt, but also that they were slaves who endured the demands of harsh taskmasters as they worked to construct the buildings which the Egyptian pharaoh required. Certainly, such information should be documented; nevertheless, there is total silence in all available historical and archaeological records. We must wonder why the Hebrews would have left the land that God originally gave to Abraham,[1] as the Bible tells us, and why they would have gone to live in a land that was not theirs. Why would they choose to become foreigners in a foreign land? Perhaps we should first go back to the

---

1 Genesis 12:1, 2

beginnings of the Hebrew people, as told in the Bible, to gain a clearer picture of what we are searching for. To do this, we will have to read between the lines of Egyptian historical records.

For the sake of order, let us chronicle the events to be discussed, beginning with how the Hebrew people found themselves in Egypt. The Bible's Book of Genesis reveals that Joseph, one of the twelve sons of Jacob and a grandson of Abraham, was sold into slavery by his jealous brothers and was taken by a caravan of Midianites to Egypt.[2] Here he encountered a series of problems including imprisonment, but the hand of God providentially moved and shaped circumstances: Joseph ultimately found himself in the Egyptian king's favor. He was even appointed vizier, second in command to Pharaoh himself.[3]

Nothing is recorded in Egyptian history about a foreigner who was appointed as the second highest official in the land of Egypt. According to the records available on the character of the Egyptians, it does not seem plausible for such an omission to exist.

The Egyptians were a people who loved games; they were playful, easygoing, full of gaiety, and free from fear.[4] They were content in their land, with little or no desire to

---

2 Genesis 37:26-28

3 Genesis 39 - 43

4 John A. Wilson, *The Burden of Egypt*, (Chicago: University of Chicago Press, 1951), p.144

extend their natural borders—the desert on the west and the Nile River on the east—with another strip of land between the latter and the Red Sea. These borders kept the people protected and self-sufficient; their sense of safety molded their nationalistic character. It is hard to imagine that such a proud group of people would have ever allowed a foreigner to rule over them. However, by the XVIII Dynasty, their character had changed[5] noticeably because an event occurred that altered their lives forever.

The peace and contentment that the Egyptians so enjoyed all their lives were suddenly shattered by the invasion of a group of foreigners, the Hyksos. These people were from an area east of Egypt, possibly Canaan. They were a Semitic people, as were the Hebrews. The Hebrews and the Hyksos shared a common ancestry since they were both descendants of Shem, one of Noah's three sons. (The word "Semite" is derived from "Shem-ite.") After the flood, Shem settled in an area encompassing the Middle East, the Arabian Peninsula, and Asia.

The Egyptians had never before needed to defend their land. They had been completely unprepared when the Hyksos suddenly invaded and easily captured them. This foreign occupation lasted about one hundred and fifty years, until the day arrived when the Egyptians rose up, defeated, and expelled their invaders.

Before the Hyksos invasion, because the Egyptians

5 J.A. Wilson, op.cit., pp.145, 146, 150.

had never needed to attack or defend themselves against intruders; and because they had never desired nor had the curiosity to explore the lands beyond their borders, their way of life had not included any military training, nor did they possess weapons of war. Their work was farming, pottery weaving, hunting, fishing, writing, serving in the palace in various capacities, and other peacetime jobs. They were not at all equipped for the invasion of the Semitic Hyksos.

The Egyptians' lack of military preparation resulted in them being easily captured. The following is a description of this invasion:

> "Something incredible and frightful befell the Nile country about 1700B.C. Suddenly, like a bolt from the blue, warriors in chariots drove into the country like arrows shot from a bow, endless columns of them in clouds of dust...Even before the Egyptians realized it, it had happened: their country was taken by surprise, overrun and vanquished...shattered under the onslaught of these Asian peoples, the 'rulers of foreign lands.' That is the meaning of the name 'Hyksos'."[6]

Although the Hyksos occupied Egypt for a relatively short time, they did leave behind several useful things: the knowledge of chariots drawn by horses and weapons used in warfare; the pride and military strength to

---

6 Werner Keller, *The Bible As History*, rev.ed. (1965: rpt. New York: William Morrow and Company, 1980), p.86

prevent another conquest of Egypt in the future; the hunger to increase their borders and conquer other peoples; a settlement near the Nile Delta of more Hebrew slaves than there were Egyptians in Egypt.

As mentioned, the reign of the Hyksos began around 1700 B.C. and lasted about one hundred and fifty years. During this time, they established dynasties and even had kings, each of whom they called Pharaoh, as was the manner of the Egyptians. They liked Egyptian ways as well as their religion and, since the latter and the state were one, the Hyksos kings believed themselves descended from the gods, as did the Egyptians. They did, however, introduce some of their own Semitic customs and religion; we find evidence of this in the fact that there was a foreign quarter in Memphis, with temples to Baal and Astarte, both Semitic gods who joined Egyptian gods in their pantheon, according to James Breasted, a famous nineteenth century Egyptologist. Breasted also states that, at the time ascribed to the Hyksos occupation, there were many Semitic words, including Hebrew words that came from the dialects of Palestine and neighboring areas. Even in later dynasties, many such words were used in Egyptian writings.[7]

There is mention of the Hyksos god, Baal, in a poem about the Battle of Kadesh, in which Ramses II is compared

---

7 James Henry Breasted, *A History of Egypt*, rev.ed., (1909: rpt. New York: Charles Scribner's Sons, 1937), p. 448

to Baal.[8] Ramses II's favorite daughter was named "Bint-Anath," which was a Semitic name meaning "Daughter of Anath"; Anath was a Syrian goddess.[9]

> "The Egyptian language also benefited from its exposure to the new horizon of Egyptian experience. A multitude of Syrian and therefore chiefly Semitic words, largely names of products unknown to the Egyptians...were fused into the language. These consisted primarily of designations for such objects as wagons and horses, weapons and implements new to Egypt..."[10]

The Hyksos looked favorably upon foreigners, especially upon the Hebrews, since they shared Semitic origins. It is not surprising, then, that Joseph found favor with these foreign invaders and their pharaoh. Regarding the appointment of Joseph to the office of vizier, the Bible and the historical records are in complete agreement. The Bible describes the ceremony by which Joseph was made viceroy or vizier, as follows:

> "And Pharaoh took off his ring from his hand, and put it upon Joseph's hand, and arrayed him in vestures of fine linen, and put a gold chain about

---

8 Adolf Erman, *Life in Ancient Egypt*, trans. H.M. Tirard, rev. ed. (1894: rpt. New York: Dover Publications, 1971), p. 394.

9 J.H. Breasted, op.cit., p.449.

10 George Steindorff and Keith C. Seele, *When Egypt Ruled the East*, rev. ed. (1942: rpt. Chicago: The University of Chicago, 1957) p.115.

his neck; and he made him to ride in the second chariot which he had; and they cried before him, 'Bow the knee' and he made him ruler over all the land of Egypt."[11]

The above description is depicted in that exact manner on Egyptian murals and reliefs. Even the fact that Joseph was given the second chariot is in accordance with the custom of that day: "The first chariot belonged to the ruler; the 'second chariot' was occupied by his chief minister."[12] It may seem unusual for a king to give a commoner such an exalted position; it was not uncommon for the Hyksos pharaoh to give his vizier enormous power and responsibilities.[13]

The Bible mentions a time of famine that came upon the surrounding lands. Egypt avoided this scarcity because Pharaoh listened to Joseph's advice obtained from God to make provision for such a time, so they had plenty of food. In gratitude, Pharaoh granted Joseph's request to bring his father, Jacob, and his eleven brothers to live in Egypt and enjoy its prosperity. He gave them land in the fertile area of the Delta, known as Goshen,[14] which explains how and why we find the Hebrews living in that very place in Egypt until the Exodus in the time of Moses.

11 Genesis 41:42, 43

12 W. Keller, op.cit., p.89

13 J.H. Breasted, op.cit., p.221

14 Genesis 45:9-11

Although the Egyptian historical records do not ascribe the events mentioned specifically to Joseph, there is evidence of Joseph's influence on the people of Egypt and of the respect he had earned from them. To this day, there is an artificial canal over two hundred miles long named after Joseph which waters the area that would otherwise have been a desert. This canal turned the land into a very fertile oasis where oranges, mandarins, peaches, olives, pomegranates, and grapes grew. It is called "Bahr Yusuf" or "Joseph's Canal," a name known throughout Egypt[15] by the fellahin—the peasants.

Accounts in the Bible and the historical records are also similar regarding significant events in life and death. Aside from celebratory events of the living, such as the ceremony during which Joseph is appointed vizier, there is correlation between the Bible's account and the historical records describing the period of mourning for the embalmed body of Jacob, Joseph's father. Information within the Bible on the embalming process aligns with the Egyptian embalming method, according to an account by Herodotus, an ancient Greek historian.[16] The biblical account found in Genesis states:

> "And Joseph commanded his servants the physicians to embalm his father: and the physicians embalmed Israel (Jacob) and forty days were

15 W. Keller, op.cit., p. 89

16 W. Keller, op.cit., p. 92

fulfilled for him; for so are fulfilled the days of those which are embalmed: and the Egyptians mourned for him threescore and ten days (70 days)."[17]

The bodies of the royalty were prepared with great care. The internal organs were removed, except for the heart, and the body cavity was then treated with various drying agents, among which was natron, a dehydrating salt. It took forty days for the body to lose its fluids, at which time it was washed and wrapped in strips of linen. Further treatments were applied so that the total length of time it took to embalm a body was seventy days.[18]

Besides the reputation that Joseph had among the Hyksos pharaohs, Jacob's name seems to have had its own influence. According to James Breasted:

"...the scarabs of a pharaoh who evidently belonged to the Hyksos time, give his name as Jacob-her or possibly Jacob-El, and it is not impossible that some chief of the Jacob-tribes of Israel for a time gained the leadership in this obscure age. Such an incident would account surprisingly well for the entrance of these tribes into Egypt, which on any hypothesis must have taken place at about this age; and in that case

---

17 Genesis 50:2, 3

18 Rita E. Freed, *Ramses II, The Great Pharaoh And His Time*, 2nd ed. (1987; rpt. Denver: Denver Museum of Natural History, n.d.) p. 105

the Hebrews in Egypt will have been but a part of the Bedouin, allies of the Kadesh or Hyksos empire..."[19]

However indirectly and by whatever deductive reasoning processes, having established the historical fact that the Hebrews did reside in the Nile Delta of Egypt at the time of the Hyksos rule, we find them there still four hundred and thirty years later,[20] under slavery.

---

19 J.H. Breasted, op.cit., p. 220

20 Exodus 12:41

Chapter II

WHEN DID THE EXODUS OCCUR?

The Bible tells us very specifically that the Hebrews would end their slavery after four hundred and thirty years. Yet, when God told Abraham that his descendants would be in Egypt for four hundred years, future enslavement and mistreatment were confirmed:

> "Know for certain that your descendants will be strangers in a country not their own, and they will be enslaved and mistreated four hundred years."[21]

There is a discrepancy between the above quotation and Exodus 12:41, where scriptures reveal that the Hebrews resided in Egypt four hundred and thirty years "to the very day," before Moses led them out. Let us investigate further to satisfy the skeptics who might question the Bible's accuracy.

Biblical references considered a "generation" to be the age of a man when his first son (from a legal standpoint) was born—in Abraham's case, one hundred years."[22]

21 Genesis 15:13

22 *The NIV Study Bible,*rev.ed. (1973; rpt. Michigan: The Zondervan

Numbers were frequently rounded off, as noted in Genesis 15:13 and in the New Testament, in Acts 7:6. However, when the actual account of the day the Exodus occurred was given, the number is exact: "to the very day."

> "Exodus 6:16-20 makes Moses the great grandson of Levi, son of Jacob and brother of Joseph. This would make four generations from Levi to Moses. But in 1 Chronicles 7:22-27 a list of ten names represents the generations between Ephraim, the son of Joseph, and Joshua. The ten generations of forty years each would equal four hundred years, the same period of time noted as our generations. But one list is abbreviated and the other gives a full genealogy."[23]

God had told Abraham that his descendants would be strangers "in a land that is not theirs." Of course, when Jacob settled in Egypt, along with his sons, seventy relatives, and servants, they were strangers in a land that was not theirs. God also said that these descendants would serve under Egyptian rulers. We now know from the biblical and archaeological accounts discussed that Jacob and his descendants lived under the reign of the Hyksos who conquered and ruled northern Egypt. We can say that the Hebrews did serve them; in fact, because they served

---

Corporation, 1985), p.28n.

23 *The NIV Study Bible,*op.cit., p. 1655n.

these kings, one might even call them "slaves." However, the Hyksos looked favorably on Joseph, on Jacob, and on the rest of the people who came into Egypt with Jacob. They were glad to welcome them because the Hyksos, too, were foreigners who shared the same Semitic roots as the Hebrews. We learned that Jacob, his sons, and seventy household members were treated well by the Hyksos and were given land in the Nile Delta, in a place called Goshen. For this reason, we can say that the time of slavery and mistreatment did not occur during the one hundred and fifty years that Egypt was ruled by the Hyksos. Therefore, we can safely assume that when the Egyptians defeated the Hyksos, they did not look kindly upon the Hebrews who lived in Goshen, who far outnumbered the Egyptians. They did not want these numerous foreigners to revolt against them. What better way to control these people than to make them into slaves working for Egyptian kings, whose job now was to restore Egypt, to expand its borders, and to build more monuments and buildings that would reflect their greatness?

Abraham's descendants were afflicted by the Egyptian kings from the time they conquered the Hyksos in 1550 B.C. until the Exodus took place. We need to determine exactly when the Hebrews left Egypt since the Bible tells us that their slavery would come to an end at a very specific time: after four hundred and thirty years. Did that time begin when Jacob and his sons entered Egypt under the Hyksos? Or did it start with Joseph's entrance into Egypt, when he was sold as a slave to Potiphar?

The Hebrew "slavery" or servitude could not have begun with Joseph's arrival into Egypt because, although he did serve under the Hyksos pharaoh, it was not long before he was appointed to the prestigious office of vizier:

> "You shall be in charge of my palace and all my people are to submit to your orders. Only with respect to the throne will I be greater than you."[24]

Serving in such a capacity would hardly qualify him to be called a slave. However, Jacob does fit the description of someone who served under foreign rulers in a land not his own. Even though under the Hyksos kings, the Hebrews were not really "slaves," they were still subjects of a foreign power. True slavery, with oppression, came after the Hyksos were overthrown.

How does this four-hundred-and-thirty-year time span align with the historical tables? Since the Hyksos ruled for one hundred and fifty years and were ousted in 1550 B.C., they began their rule in 1700 B.C. Jacob's arrival into Egypt along with his eleven sons must have taken place during that time. We can begin to count the time of Hebrew slavery from Jacob's settlement in Egypt along with the seventy relatives and servants, and his eleven sons—the forefathers of the Hebrew nation. In fact, God told Jacob:

---

24 Genesis 41:40

"...I am God, the God of thy father: fear not to go down into Egypt; for I will there make of thee a great nation."[25]

Four hundred and thirty years elapsed from the time that Jacob and these first members of the Hebrew people settled in Egypt, in Goshen—the land given to them by Pharaoh—until the Exodus. The Bible tells us that Jacob lived in Egypt for seventeen years. When he died, his body was embalmed in the Egyptian fashion and his family was permitted to bury him in the land of Canaan.

"And Pharaoh said, 'Go up, and bury thy father, according as he made thee swear.' And Joseph went up to bury his father: and with him went up all the servants of the elders of his house, and all the elders of the land of Egypt, and all the house of Joseph, and his brethren and his father's house...and there went up with him both chariots and horsemen: and it was a very great company."[26]

Here is further proof that this event could not have happened under Egyptian rule: The Egyptian pharaohs would not have permitted a Hebrew slave to be embalmed; nor would they have allowed all of Jacob's relatives and servants, as well as all the elders of the land, to

---

25 Gen. 46:3

26 Gen. 50:6-9

leave Egypt to bury Jacob in Canaan. This could only have occurred during the reign of the Hyksos. For this reason, to determine how long Jacob lived in Egypt before his death, we must stay within the confines of the time of the Hyksos rule there.

We can now calculate just when the Hebrew slavery began and ended. To arrive at this conclusion, we need to know when Jacob, his family and his servants and flocks went down into Egypt. The following charts display the information the Bible gives us in Genesis, Chapters 39 to 41: the number of years, ages, dates, and additions and subtractions, in a format that might be easier to understand at a glance. Having this information in chart form, we can refer to it throughout our reading of *Genesis 15:13*, should we become overwhelmed or confused by the numbers we need to add or subtract as we navigate the text.

Chart 1
Jacob's Possible Earliest Arrival in Egypt

Summary of facts from the Bible to determine Jacob's earliest arrival into Egypt, marking the beginning of Hebrew slavery:

- Joseph was sold as a slave at age --- 17 years

- Joseph was in prison (after working for Potiphar) for --- 2 years

- Joseph was rewarded (interpreted Pharaoh's dreams) at age --- 30 years

- Joseph worked for Potiphar --- 11 years

- The years of plenty --- 7 years

- The years of famine, when Jacob arrived in Egypt --- 2 years

- Joseph's age when Jacob came to Egypt --- 39 years

- Time elapsed from Joseph's and Jacob's entry into Egypt --- 22 years

- Hyksos began to rule --- 1700 BC

- Exodus 12:40 reveals the time the Hebrews were in Egypt --- 430 years

- Jacob's earliest arrival in Egypt (1700 – 22= 1678) --- 1678 BC

- Earliest date for the Exodus (1678 – 430 = 1248) --- 1248 BC

(NOTE: The reign of Ramses II was from 1279 BC to 1213 BC)

_____

Chart 2
Jacob's Latest Possible Arrival in Egypt

Summary of facts from the Bible to determine the latest date for Jacob's arrival into Egypt, marking the beginning of Hebrew slavery:

- Hyksos rule ended --- 1550 BC
- Jacob's sojourn in Egypt before his death --- 17 years
- Joseph's age at Jacob's arrival --- 39 years
- Joseph's death at age --- 110 years
- Time elapsed between Jacob's arrival and Joseph's death --- 71 years
- Latest date for Jacob's arrival in Egypt (1550 + 71 = 1621) --- 1621 BC
- Latest date for the Exodus (1621 - 430 = 1191 B.C.) --- 1191 BC

(NOTE: Reign of Siptah was from 1194 BC to 1188 BC)

If we assume that Jacob entered Egypt at the beginning of the Hyksos's Dynasty, the earliest time for this would have been during 1678 BC. Chart 1 explains the calculation of this date. Before that year, Joseph would not have been able to intercede for his family before Pharaoh as an official in the king's court. Therefore, it wasn't until Joseph was thirty-nine years old that Jacob and his sons, wives, children, and servants entered Egypt.

The Bible tells us that Joseph was seventeen years old when his brothers sold him as a slave to Potiphar, one of Pharaoh's officials. Joseph was brought into Egypt and worked for his master until he was unjustly accused of rape by Potiphar's wife. Because of that accusation, he was imprisoned for two years. During that time, he interpreted the dreams of two other prisoners, a cupbearer to the king and a baker. When word of this reached Pharaoh, he sent for Joseph to interpret a dream he'd had. By God's revelation, Joseph told Pharaoh what the dream meant: There would be seven years of plenty in Egypt, followed by seven years of famine. Pharaoh rewarded Joseph by appointing him as vizier or second in command over all of Egypt.[27]

We do not know exactly how long Joseph was employed by Potiphar; however, based on information found in Chart 1, we can make some calculations that lead us to believe Joseph worked in his master's house for at least eleven years before being imprisoned. Referring again to Chart 1, we can see that by adding the seven years of plenty plus the two years into the famine when Jacob came

---

27 Genesis, chapters 39-41

into Egypt, we find that Joseph was about thirty-nine years old at that time.

Twenty-two years had passed since he was sold by his brothers. Referencing Chart 1, we can see that if we subtract these twenty-two years from the year the Hyksos conquered the throne of Egypt, 1700 BC, we see the year 1678 BC as the time for Jacob's arrival into Egypt. Four hundred and thirty years later, the time of the Exodus, would have been the year 1248 BC, the time when an Egyptian, Ramses II, was the king.

The calculations found in Chart 2 are there only to show how Jacob could not have arrived in Egypt toward the end of Hyksos rule. We have already mentioned that Egyptian kings would not have permitted a foreigner to be embalmed or to be placed in a coffin in Egypt.[28] There is additional support for this proposition: based on the numbers given in the Bible, adding and subtracting as seen in Chart 2 would bring us to the year 1191 BC as the latest date for the Exodus. This is not possible because Israel was already settled in Palestine by 1208 BC, as mentioned in a document which is engraved on the "Israel Stela (stone)" stone. This would indicate that the Exodus would have taken place at least forty years before the date of that stela, the duration of time the Hebrews wandered in the wilderness.

"Indeed, in ancient Egyptian records, the people

28 Gen. 50:26

of Israel are mentioned only once, on a stela inscribed in Year 5 of the reign of Ramses II's son and successor, Merneptah. Erected in commemoration of a victory over the Libyans, the so-called 'Israel Stela' also lists all the cities and tribes in Syria and Canaan that Merneptah had similarly defeated. The fact that Israel is so listed provides clear (and significant) evidence that by the fifth year after the death of Ramses II, the desert wanderings of the people of Israel had ended. Assuming forty years for these wanderings, if the Exodus took place at least forty years prior to the Israel Stela and no more than seventy-one (sixty-six years of Ramses II's rule plus five years of Merneptah's), then the departure from Egypt would have occurred during Ramses the Great's regency. Accordingly, Ramses the Great and Moses may have been contemporaries."[29]

The Israel Stela must have been carved a while after Joshua led the Hebrews into the "promised land." This tangible stone document makes it possible for us to say with certainty that Jacob did not arrive in Egypt toward the end of the reign of the Hyksos pharaohs. Instead, we should focus on his possible arrival at the beginning or middle of the foreign rule.

Chart 3 shows further calculations using the

29 R.E. Freed, op.cit., p. 77.

information on the Israel Stela to determine the date of the end of Hebrew slavery.

Chart 3
The Year of the Exodus and the Israel Stela

- Reign of Merneptah began --- 1213 BC
- Fifth year of his reign when Israel Stela was inscribed --- 1208 BC
- The Hebrews wandered in the wilderness for --- 40 years
- Exodus occurred at least 40 years before the Israel Stela was inscribed --- 1248 BC

(NOTE: This date coincides exactly with the date for Jacob's earliest arrival in Egypt, found in Chart 1. Ramses II was Pharaoh during this time from 1279 BC to 1213 BC)

As we can see, Chart 1 and Chart 3 align as to 1248 BC being the year that the Exodus took place, during the reign of Ramses II. Chart 1 examines Jacob's earliest possible arrival in Egypt, along with his sons, the descendants of Abraham—an event that would mark the beginning of the four hundred and thirty years of Hebrew slavery. This chart arrives at the year 1248 BC for the end of Hebrew slavery in Egypt.

Chart 3 uses the Israel Stela, which mentions Israel as a nation and which was written in the fifth year of Merneptah, 1208 BC. Deducting the forty years for the Hebrews' time in the wilderness, following the Exodus, the date for the latter is 1248 BC. What is the probability that the same year could be arrived at from two entirely different directions on the timeline, four hundred and ninety-two years apart, and from information obtained from two unique sources?

According to Webster's Dictionary, probability is defined as "a mathematical basis for prediction that, for an exhaustive set of outcomes, is the ration of the outcomes that would produce a given event to the total number of possible outcomes." The definition continues to say that it is "a logical relation between statements such that evidence confirming one confirms the other to some degree."

If this book had been written by a mathematician, the rate of probability for the above findings would be included here. However, in the absence of such a rate, we can still say that it would seem impossible that several random variables should converge upon the same event by chance. Rather than thinking that such a date could be arrived at by accident, the facts would lead us to say that the precise year for the Hebrew Exodus from Egypt has been left for us to determine from the indirect information obtained from the Bible and from the Israel Stela.

These two sources each confirm the data contained in the other by providing more than one variable that points to the same date. For the skeptic, the historical record probably carries a good deal of credibility. When the historical record agrees with information found in the Bible, even the skeptic might be convinced of the accuracy of the Bible.

Since the Bible told us explicitly that the Exodus would take place four hundred and thirty years "to the day," it should not come as a surprise that the Bible has provided enough information for us to be able to arrive at the exact date, when combining this information with the historical events recorded in the Israel Stela.

We know from the Bible that the Exodus took place on the day after the first Passover. The Bible tells us that Passover is to be celebrated on the fifteenth day of Nissan, the Hebrew month that corresponds to our March/April. The Hebrew day begins at sundown and ends at the next sundown. On the evening of the fifteenth day of Nissan, the tenth plague came upon Egypt, killing all the first-born of the households that did not have the blood of the lamb on the doorposts and lintels. Death "passed over" the households where the blood of the lamb was brushed on the doorposts and lintels, as God had instructed Moses to tell all the people to do to avoid this plague—including the Egyptians. Early the next morning, still the fifteenth day of Nissan, in his grief, Pharaoh ordered that the Hebrews leave Egypt; they departed in haste, and were led by Moses.[30] Thus, we can know that the Exodus took place on exactly the fifteenth day of Nissan, in the year 1248 BC.

---

30 Exodus 12:6-42

Chapter III

THE EGYPTIAN PHARAOHS RETURN

Having established the veracity of the Bible regarding the beginning of Hebrew slavery, its end four hundred and thirty years later, to the day—the fifteenth day of Nissan, 1248 BC—let us return to the overthrow of the Hyksos, foreigners who ruled Egypt for one hundred and fifty years. These Asiatic rulers of Egypt, having Semitic origins in common with the Hebrews, had lived in harmony with them for that time. The Hyksos were defeated by an Egyptian army from Thebes, and, after their defeat, the true time of slavery with affliction began for the Hebrews.

In the year 1550 BC, the Egyptians regained rule of their land when their Pharaoh Kamose, followed by his brother Ahmose I, defeated the Hyksos.[31] It is hardly surprising that any foreigner was looked upon with mistrust. Gone was the innocence that the Egyptians had once had

---

31 K.A. Kitchen, *Pharaoh Triumphant, The Life and Times of Ramesses II, King of Egypt*, 3rd ed. (1982; Warminster, England: Aris & Phillips Ltd., 1985), p.9.

when they enjoyed peace in their land. They now looked with suspicion and fear upon the Hebrews who, during their prosperous coexistence with the Hyksos, had so multiplied that their number exceeded that of the Egyptian population. The Egyptians feared that these Semitic people could rise up against them, just as the Hyksos had done. They feared that this vast multitude might join any foreign invader crossing their boundaries in an attempt at another overthrow. These fears led a series of pharaohs to impose control over the Hebrews by oppressing them as slaves.

During the period of four hundred and thirty years, except for the time when the Hyksos ruled, there were some Egyptian kings who were very harsh and some who were less so. Most likely, Ahmose I, the first Egyptian pharaoh to rule after the Hyksos were defeated, was the first pharaoh who oppressed the Hebrews because he "knew not Joseph."[32] He either really knew nothing about Joseph because he had lived in Thebes, which was far from where the Hyksos had ruled, or he chose to disregard any respect for Joseph's memory. After all, Joseph had been the most powerful viceroy, second only to Pharaoh, according to the Bible. After the throne of Egypt had been regained, each subsequent pharaoh "knew not Joseph." This obviously meant that the Hebrews no longer had the special treatment they had been accorded by their fellow

---

32 Exodus 1:8

Semites, but rather were looked upon as a great multitude of "foreigners" who might pose a danger to their regained Egyptian rule.

The worst time of oppression for the Hebrew slaves began when there arose yet another pharaoh "who knew not Joseph." According to the Bible, this king saw the ever-growing Hebrew population as a threat and sought to control it by having its newborn males killed at birth by the midwives—a plan that eventually failed.[33] Pharaoh then gave the order to all his people that every Hebrew child born must be thrown into the Nile.[34] Moses was one of those babies destined to be killed; but, by the providential hand of God, he was protected and then adopted by "Pharaoh's own daughter."[35]

Egyptologists, historians, and theologians all disagree to varying degrees as to who the pharaoh of the oppression and of the Exodus might have been. Some think it could have been Thutmose III (1479-1425 BC). Others name Merneptah (1213-1204 BC). Still one other, Immanuel Velikovski, writes that, while agreeing that it might have been RamsesII who was the pharaoh of the Exodus, he said that this pharaoh was a contemporary of Nebuchadnezzar, king of Babylon.[36] This would be

---

33 Exodus 1:18

34 Exodus 1:22

35 Exodus 2:2-10

36 Immanuel Velikovski, *Ramses II and His Time*, (New York: Double-

impossible since the Babylonian king reigned from 605 to 562 BC.[37]

Although we have already established the time of the Exodus and are now certain that Ramses II was the pharaoh at that time, we need to ascertain who the pharaoh of the oppression might have been. We even need to investigate and determine if the pharaoh of the Exodus and of the oppression were one and the same person.

As if we were still searching for the pharaoh of the Exodus, let us approach this entire subject from a different perspective to become even more astonished at the probability of a third confirmation for the time of the Exodus. The legitimate reason for this: The more information we can obtain from different sources confirming our findings, the more certain we can be that these findings are correct. In conducting this research, we hope to also determine the pharaoh of the oppression.

Again, the Bible provides certain data that can be backed by additional historical evidence, pinpointing the time of the Exodus and, hence, the Egyptian ruler at that time, while approaching the subject from a different point of view.

One of the ten plagues—that of frogs—speaks of

day & Company, Inc., 1978), p. 184.

37 *Encyclopaedia Britannica*, vol. 16, rev.ed., (1929; rpt. Chicago: William Benton, Publisher, 1961), p. 185.

ovens, kneading troughs, bowls, and pots.[38] It is an archaeological and historical fact that these items were introduced in the XIX Dynasty (1327 to 1188 BC), not before or after it:

> "With the New Kingdom bread ovens were introduced to replace the earlier process of baking in mounds over an open hearth, and earthenware stoves about three feet high for general cooking...and the food was boiled in earthenware saucepans or grilled on a spit."[39]

Another fact, verified in historical records, is that the army did not become as vastly organized, nor did it have numbers so large in their ranks, nor was there such a wide use of chariots and horses until the XIX Dynasty.[40] Exodus 14:9 tells us:

> "But the Egyptians pursued after them, all the horses and chariots of Pharaoh..."

One last item helps to identify the time: even though gold was used in temple worship before the XIX Dynasty, it was not used as widely in personal jewelry and ornaments, such as rings, bracelets, and earrings, except in the royal household, until the XIX Dynasty.[41] The Bible states:

---

38 Exodus 8:3

39 R.R. Sellman, *Ancient Egypt*, (New York: Roy Publisher,`960) p. 52

40 George Steindorff and Keith C. Seele, op.cit., p.91.

41 Waley-el-dine Sameh, *Daily Life In Ancient Egypt*, (n.p.: "Short Re-

"Speak now in the ears of the people, and let every man borrow of his neighbour and every woman of her neighbour, jewels of silver, and jewels of gold. And the Lord gave the people favour in the sight of the Egyptians."[42]

Since the evidence just mentioned seems to narrow our search to the XIX Dynasty, we will concentrate on the pharaohs who reigned during that time. Chart 4 follows and lists these pharaohs.

Chart 4
Pharaohs of the XVIII and the XIX Dynasties

The end of the XVIII Dynasty (1550-1295 B.C.)

Haremhab -------- 1327-1295 BC

The XIX Dynasty (1295-1187 B.C.)

Ramses I -------- 1295 - 1294 BC

Seti I -------- 1294 - 1279 BC

Ramses II -------- 1279 - 1213 BC

Merneptah -------- 1213 - 1204 BC

Amenmesses -------- 1204 - 1200 BC

---

cords" Publisher, 1964), p. 96.

42 Exodus 11:2, 3.

The Moses Gap

Seti II ------- 1200 - 1194 BC

Siptah ------- 1194 - 1188 BC

Queen Tewosret -------- 1188 - 1187 BC

Keeping these dates and people in mind, we can begin our search within the confines of the reign of these pharaohs, a total of about 145 years. We will deliberately omit Ramses III because he belonged to the XX Dynasty, although he carried the Ramesside name. Unless we cannot find what we are looking for in the XIX Dynasty, we will not need to travel that far into the era of more modern Egyptian history.

One of the pharaohs of the XIX Dynasty could have been the pharaoh mentioned in the Bible as having so oppressed the Hebrew slaves with his unreasonable demands for building that he may have been the one who precipitated the events of the Exodus. This tells us that we need to concentrate on the kings who were builders. To narrow the field further, we will have to eliminate the "warrior" pharaohs since they would have been away on the battlefield and would not have required the use of a large slave force for the task of building.

Chapter IV

THE PHARAOH WHO "KNEW NOT JOSEPH"

Why is it so important to know with certainty which pharaoh was the one of the oppression and which was the one of the Exodus? Why have we spent so much time and effort in researching the different possibilities? The Bible does not record the names of the pharaohs involved and the dates of their rule. If we are to attempt to place Moses in a historical time frame, we must know the precise historical Egyptian kings to whom the Bible refers. The main message of the Book of Exodus is God's deliverance of His people from the hand of their enemies. Its purpose is not to record historical events but to mention them where necessary, in the presentation of the relationship between God and His people. Yet, for those of us with a curiosity to know historical details about these events as mentioned in the Bible so that we can pursue the purpose of this book, these details become very important.

We have followed various "rabbit trails," as my pastor and friend used to say. Nevertheless, the investigation of each of these trails has been necessary in order to provide historical details that support the goal of this work. As a refresher, we must ask and answer: "What is the purpose of this book?" It is to fill in the "Moses gap," the gap—which could even be called an abyss—that exists between the Bible and the historical records.

In exploring the pharaohs of the XIX Dynasty, we discovered there were some who could be called "warriors" and others, "builders." There were some pharaohs of the first category who, when they were not away at war, were at home busily building. Some examples of these pharaohs include Haremhab, an army general who began his reign as Pharaoh when he was in his sixties. He was not a XIX Dynasty king but was the last of the XVIII Dynasty pharaohs. He is mentioned here because he played a significant role in our research, as will be seen in other chapters.

While he ruled Egypt, Haremhab brought his involvement in the battlefield to an end and turned his attention fully to the restoration of Egypt. He and his contemporary, Ay, who had been king before him, were instrumental in ending the damage that Akhenaten, later known as the "heretic king," had brought upon Egypt. Akhenaten had ordered the destruction of images and statues of Egyptian gods and, in their place, had promoted the worship of one god called Aten or the Aten disk, which was the sun. His attitude in ruling was quite relaxed; consequently, much of the land that had belonged to Egypt was lost to foreign invaders. The pharaohs who followed Akhenaten and who continued his ways were Smenkhkare and Tutankhamun, the boy king who started his reign at the age of nine.

Haremhab was determined to restore the worship of the ancient Egyptian gods, and to rebuild temples, sculptures, and reliefs that had been destroyed during the "Amarna Age." This age had introduced a new form of art—elongated figures that represented Akhenaten, his wife, Nefertiti, and their three daughters.

Haremhab focused on restoring things to the way they had been before Akhenaten's rule—things such as law and order, respect for and worship of all the Egyptian gods, and the authority of the office of Pharaoh.

Haremhab's protégé, Ramses I, the first pharaoh of the new Dynasty, also gained the throne in his later years and became another warrior-turned-builder. His building career lasted not quite two years due to poor health that brought his reign—and his life—to an abrupt end. His son, Seti I, picked up where his father left off. When he was not fighting battles, he was at the palace directing the building of monuments, tombs, and temples.

> "The almost annual summer campaigns, however, occupied only a few brief weeks each year, two or three months at the most. Otherwise, Sethos I (Seti I) was well occupied with routine administration at home, and in celebrating the

major festivals of the great gods...And occupied, too, with the other half of his twin ambition—to equal in size and magnificence the great buildings of his other model, Amenhophis II."[43]

As we can see, Seti I was responsible for large-scale building projects: parts of the Temple of Karnak; his memorial temple on the west bank; his tomb at Deir el Medina, in the Valley of the Kings; a shrine to the god Osiris, in Abydos; a summer palace in the Delta; new work in Heliopolis and Memphis--in the old temples to the gods Re and Ptah respectively. He even indulged his young son's desire to build a temple to Osiris at Abydos, although on a smaller scale than his own.[44]

Seti I fulfilled his ambition to surpass the work of other builder-pharaohs before him. However, it was the next builder, his son Ramses II, who stood out among XIX Dynasty builders and among all other pharaohs before or after him. It is said that Ramses II was responsible for the building of one half of the surviving monuments seen in Egypt today.[45]

Imagine how the loyal taskmasters must have pressured the slave laborers! It took three thousand years to produce the first half of the buildings that survive in our

43 K.A. Kitchen, op.cit., p.25.

44 K.A. Kitchen, op.cit., p. 37

45 Veronica Ions, *Egyptian Mythology*, (London: Hamlyn, 1968), p. 123.

present age. Yet, these slaves were expected to fulfill the enormous quotas required in the building of the other half of Egypt's existing tombs and temples. Additionally, this massive work had to be completed during the sixty-six-year reign of one pharaoh, Ramses II. Into what frenetic endeavors the slaves must have been forced!

> "Forty overseers were each required to deliver two thousand bricks according to the inscription on a roll of leather written in Ramses II's fifth regnal year."[46]

The Bible tells us that the slaves had to obtain straw to make the bricks.[47] This method of making bricks is perfectly accurate. In the British Museum, there is a brick that was made during the reign of Ramses II, with his "cartouche"—his name, written in hieroglyphs and enclosed in an oval. It is approximately a foot and a half in length and made of greenish mud and straw. There is a caption underneath:

> "Brick made of Nile mud and chopped chaff stamped with the name of King Ramses II. It probably came from one of the brick buildings which form part of the Ramesseum, the funerary temple of Ramses."[48]

46 R.E. Freed, op.cit., p. 76.

47 Exodus 5:7

48 British Museum, Egyptian Hall, Room 63, Exhibit Number 6020, Gift of Lord Prudhoe, 1835.

The process of making bricks must have been very time consuming. First, the straw was gathered, then it was mixed with mud, put in a mold, and set out in the sun to dry.

> "When King Ramesses II began to build his favourite town of Ramesses (generally called Pi-Ramessu by the Egyptians) and the warehouses of Pithom, he gathered the Israelites, set gang masters over them and forced them 'with hard bondage' to mould bricks. As work, it was tedious, but not all that difficult. Nile mud was mixed with sand and chopped straw, and to obtain the right consistency, the substance had to be moistened, trodden out for a long time and stirred at intervals with a mattock. The workman exactly filled his mould, which stood close beside him, with the damp compound, removing any surplus with a wooden scraper, and then quickly lifted it off, thus leaving the brick intact. After being left to dry for eight days, it was ready for use. For choice, brick makers settled to work near a pool and water carriers kept them supplied with water. Other workers would go and collect the stubble from the harvested fields, in order to prepare the chopped straw. Pharaoh's order to the children of Israel to go and fetch their own straw, without reducing their daily

quota of manufactured bricks, was a very real additional hardship, but grumbling would only have meant a beating from the gang masters. The bricks were carried on a pair of flat trays slung like a yoke."[49]

In order to carry out a building program of such enormous size over a relatively short period of time—less than Ramses II's lifetime—large numbers of laborers were needed. How convenient that, practically next door to the building sites of Pithom and Ramses, in Goshen, there lived Hebrew slaves whose population outnumbered that of the Egyptians.

Why not oppress these people to keep them in subservience, lest they revolt against their masters and overpower them? After all, were they not close friends of the hated Hyksos, the enemy that held Egypt in humiliation for about one hundred and fifty years?

Renowned Egyptologist James Breasted said that Ramses II was unable to use Asiatic slaves for his building projects as extensively as his predecessors had.[50] However, since Tanis is where Ramses II's most frequently used palace was located and since it was near Goshen in the Nile Delta, it is logical to assume he would have availed himself

49 Pierre Montet, *Everyday Life In Egypt, In The Days Of Ramesses The Great*, trans. A.R. Maxwell-Hyslop and Margaret S. Drower, 3rd ed. (1958; rpt. Philadelphia: University of Pennsylvania Press, 1981), pp. 161, 162.

50 J. Breasted, op.cit., pp. 446, 447.

of the large Hebrew slave population. Tanis was also near the biblical Pithom, which appears in Egyptian inventories as Per-Itum, "House of the god Atum," and does not go back further in time than the reign of Ramses II.[51] The most likely choice for slaves in building Pithom and the nearby store city of Raamses, previously known as Avaris,[52] would have been the Hebrew people residing in Goshen. Another source also places Pithom in the delta region:

> "Swiss Egyptologist Edouard Naville...In January, 1883, conducted the fund's first dig (Egypt Exploration Fund) at Tell es Maskhuta, in the delta. His success was instant. Within weeks the committee learned that two statues had been found, a falcon and a seated scribe, both of which bore the ancient name of the site—Pithom."[53]

As we synthesize all the information discussed on this matter, we might be justified in confidently assuming that Ramses II was the king whose oppression of the Hebrew slaves resulted in the biblical confrontation with Moses. Ramses matches the Bible's description of a king who was an oppressor who "knew not Joseph." But, as we shall see, he was only one of several who, since the expulsion of the Hyksos, "knew not Joseph."

The Bible says:

51 W. Keller, op.cit., pp. 110,111.

52 W. Keller, op.cit.,p.111.

53 Christine Hobson, *The World Of The Pharaohs*, (n.p., n.d.) p. 40.

"Now there arose up a new king over Egypt, which knew not Joseph. And he said unto his people, behold, the people of the children of Israel are more and mightier than we: Come on, let us deal wisely with them; lest they multiply, and it come to pass, that when there falleth out any war, they join also unto our enemies, and fight against us, and so get them up out of the land. Therefore, they did set over them taskmasters to afflict them with their burdens, and they built for Pharaoh treasure cities, Pithom and Raamses."[54]

Although the latter part of the above quote refers to Ramses II building the treasure cities, the rest of it applies to him and to other pharaohs who preceded him who equally "knew not Joseph." Whether there was a king who "knew not Joseph" literally or figuratively, either case can be substantiated. It is well to note here that when the Egyptians did not change the truth to flatter themselves, they quite readily practiced "out of sight, out of mind." They simply ceased to speak of anything unpleasant as if it had never existed. Names were gouged out from monuments and replaced by other names, carved or painted over the original ones. In a similar manner, names were obliterated from the thoughts of the Egyptians by never being mentioned again. The Egyptian belief was that to

---

54 Exodus 1:8-11.

remove a name or to cease to speak it was to kill the soul of its owner, as mentioned in the following quote:

> "The writing of a man's name could perpetuate his memory; its subsequent destruction pro-duced the contrary result.[55]

The fact that a pharaoh did not know Joseph could very well mean that he chose not to remember there was ever such a man who occupied the second most powerful position in Egypt at a time in their history which was best forgotten, as far as the Egyptians were concerned.

Literally, the period of Hyksos rule was such an embarrassment to the Egyptians that they did not refer to this time lapse of one hundred and fifty years in any of their historical records, paintings, or carvings:

> "When we come to the Hyksos themselves, we face a baffling phenomenon: the absence of contemporary written records. If this conquest were as critical to the course of Egyptian culture as we claim, how could Egyptian writings have blanketed it with silence? The answer lies in the nature and purpose of Egyptian texts, which as-serted the eternal, and not the ephemeral and which presented for eternity those aspects of life which were felt to represent most truly the gods' purposes in Egypt. In that psychology, there

55 T.G.H. James, *Pharaoh's People*, 2nd ed. (1948; rpt. Chicago: University of Chicago Press, 1984), p.133.

was no impulse for writing down the record of a great national humiliation; that record would come when and as the Hyksos were successfully expelled."[56]

Silence exists about the time when a people, who so adopted Egyptian ways that they called their king "Pharaoh" and worshiped Egyptian gods, chose to appoint a Hebrew named Joseph as second in command over all of Egypt. So, it is very likely that a couple of centuries after the defeat of the Hyksos and about four hundred years since the time of Joseph, Ramses II might never have heard the name of Joseph or known anything about him.

Figuratively, Ramses II might have known such things by word of mouth. There is a list of kings in Turin, in front of which Seti I and his son, Ramses, are depicted, which contains the names of some Hyksos pharaohs— although there is no mention that they were foreigners. It was not until later that sources identified these names as Hyksos kings.[57] Perhaps, in his nationalistic pride, Ramses II might have chosen to forget such a time and, therefore, did not acknowledge Joseph—especially the favor he and his family enjoyed in Egypt. Ramses II was a true Egyptian who looked down on anyone who was not Egyptian. Therefore, it was certain that many Hebrew slaves were not going to enjoy his favor. Apart from pride

56 J.A.Wilson, op.cit., p.133

57 T.G.H. James, op.cit., p.133.

in their land, Egyptians looked down on shepherds,[58] which added another negative point to their opinion of the Hebrew people, whose livelihood before slavery had been provided by shepherding.

The friends of the Hyksos, the Hebrews, probably became slaves as soon as the Hyksos were expelled. They disliked and mistrusted the Egyptians, who kept an enormous group of people under their control while deriving free labor from them. There was not one pharaoh of the oppression and one of the Exodus, as many scholars would have us believe. Reviewing the historical facts, we can see that the period of true Hebrew slavery began in 1550 B.C. with the takeover of power by the Egyptians.

It continued during the time of massive building under various pharaohs, among whom were Haremhab, Ramses I, and Seti I—and culminated under Ramses II. Seventeen Egyptian pharaohs ruled during this time. Those who were builders drove the slaves harder, although the Hebrew slaves shared the burden with other Asiatic slaves until the time of Ramses II, as previously mentioned.

Those who were warriors did not require the services of their slaves as extensively as the builders did. As has been mentioned, half of the buildings we see in Egypt today date from the time of Ramses II. It is therefore reasonable to assume that this must have been the period when

---

58 Genesis 46:34.

the Hebrews, who were alone in serving their masters, must have endured the greatest hardships. It is natural, then, that such a people would turn to their God for help in their time of trouble:

> "And it came to pass in the process of time that the king of Egypt died: and the children of Israel (another name for the Hebrew population) sighed by reason of the bondage, and they cried, and their cry came up unto God by reason of the bondage."[59]

Thus, we see that there were several pharaohs who might have been considered oppressors, the first being Ahmose I, who completed the overthrow of the Hyksos ten years after his accession. He is probably the first pharaoh "who knew not Joseph." Then, following the rule of several pharaohs, there was one who, intimidated by the large number of Hebrews, decided to cut down their population while seeking to defeat their strong spirit, ordering the death of every male Hebrew child.[60]

While there were many oppressors, there is significant evidence that identifies Ramses II as the worst of the oppressors; he was the one who oversaw construction of the most buildings in a relatively short period of time. He is accurately described as a pharaoh whose oppression of slaves was so terrible that it precipitated the events

59 Exodus 2:23.

60 Exodus 1:16-22.

culminating in the Exodus, which occurred during his reign. There are some who agree that he was an oppressor, but say that the pharaoh of the Exodus was his son, Merneptah. This is chronologically impossible as the Israel Stela, the previously mentioned stone document, proves. There is also evidence that Ramses II especially oppressed the Hebrews in his middle years. Our research will later reveal that he was fifty-six years of age at the time of the Exodus.

> "In Ramesses II's middle years, we read of 'soldiers and the Apiru' (Habiru, in cuneiform sources) (Hebrews?) who are dragging stone for the great pylon-gateway of Ramesses II."[61]

According to the Bible, one of the stipulations Pharaoh made because of Moses's request to let the Hebrew people go was to worsen their oppression by making their labor not only harder, but also impossible:

> "Then the slave drivers and the foremen went out and said to the people, 'This is what Pharaoh says: I will not give you any more straw. Go and get your own straw wherever you can find it, but your work will not be reduced at all.' So the people scattered all over Egypt to gather stubble to use for straw."[62]

61 K.A. Kitchen, op.cit., p. 70.

62 Exodus 5:10-12.

Earlier, we learned how difficult and lengthy a process it was to make bricks in those days; we can now better understand how impossible it would have been to fulfill the daily quota of bricks if the people had to gather the straw or stubble themselves. The Bible continues:

> "Then the Israelite foremen went and appealed to Pharaoh: 'Why have you treated your servants this way? Your servants are given no straw, yet we are told, 'Make bricks! Your servants are being beaten, but the fault is with your own people.'"[63]

From this text, we can almost visualize the Hebrew slaves, driven by the Egyptian taskmasters to produce the same quota of bricks as when the Egyptians provided the straw, having to gather the straw themselves. They were forced into giving up putting even stubble into the Nile mud mixture to cut down on the time. This leads to another source of information that provides us with a most startling archaeological discovery, one that should close any argument about who the pharaoh of the Exodus was. There is one building, among others in Pithom from the time of Ramses II's reign, which was found to have been built using three different types of brick:

> "In 1883, the treasure or store cities of Pitum and Raames were unearthed, and details of their

---

63 Exodus 5:15-18.

construction noted. It was seen that the lower courses of the walls were made of usual sun-dried mud bricks in which chopped-up straw had been mixed for binding the clay together and strengthening it. In the middle courses, the bricks lacked straw, but contained stubble and roots of the grain crop, which the labourers had put in to take the place of straw. It appears as if they had put in whatever they could find handy. The top courses contained neither straw nor stubble. This shows a resemblance to what we read in Exodus 1:8, 11...Exodus 5:6-8, 10-14."[64]

The above information strongly supports the biblical account; we can have no doubt that it was Ramses II who oppressed the Hebrews above and beyond any oppression they had suffered until the time of his reign. It also confirms what the Bible tells us about Pharaoh's response to Moses's request to let the people go. This places Ramses II in the sequence just prior to the Exodus, during the time that God allowed the plagues to descend upon Egypt because of Pharaoh's refusal to heed Moses and his elder brother, Aaron.

---

64 H.V. Morsley, *Junior Bible Archaeology*, (New York: Roy Publishers, Inc., 1963), pp.47, 48.

Chapter V

The Pharaoh of the Oppression

Although we seem to be overlapping information about the pharaoh of the oppression and the pharaoh of the Exodus, there is a logical reason for this: When we were searching for the year the Exodus took place (1248 BC, according to the Israel Stela), we also found the pharaoh who was on the throne at that time, Ramses II—thus solving that part of the puzzle. When we were searching for data on the pharaoh of the oppression, we had to travel along an imaginary timeline to pinpoint the Dynasty during which he might have ruled so we could concentrate on it. Once we knew that most of the facts given in the Bible about this period pointed to the XIX Dynasty, we could then ascertain the identity of the pharaoh of the oppression.

Because of the enormous slave population needed for Ramses II's colossal building projects, and the fact that he was the only ruler who used Hebrew slaves exclusively, it was easy to conclude that he was the ruler during the oppression that led to the Exodus. However, he was not the pharaoh who decreed that all male Hebrew babies be put to death. We need to go back in time to discover the identity of that pharaoh.

Since Ramses II was the pharaoh at the time of the Exodus, we know that he was a contemporary of Moses. At his accession to the throne in 1279 BC, he was twenty-five years old. In 1248 BC, at the time of the Exodus, when the Bible tells us Moses was eighty years old, Ramses II was fifty-six years of age—twenty-four years younger than Moses. Obviously, he could not have been the despot who ordered the death of the male Hebrew babies because Moses was one of those babies.[65] The pharaoh who ordered such an edict had to be one of Ramses II's predecessors.

As mentioned previously, several pharaohs tyrannized the slaves at different times; the more these pharaohs wanted to accomplish architecturally, the more they mistreated the slaves. The pharaoh mentioned in the beginning of the Book of Exodus as one who afflicted and persecuted the Hebrews may have been Ahmose I, the first pharaoh "who knew not Joseph." He was the pharaoh on the throne when the Hyksos were overthrown, in 1550 BC. The one who demanded the death of the Hebrew male children reigned over one hundred years later, in 1328 BC, the year of Moses's birth. Finding this year would have been an almost impossible task, were it

---

65 Exodus 1:15-20

not for the Israel Stela, which we have already discussed. Such information simplifies our search considerably.

The Bible tells us that Moses's parents hid him for three months and then set him out in the bulrushes of the Nile River, under his sister's watchful eye.[66] We know that this situation had not existed three years prior to Moses's birth, during the last year of Tutankhamun's reign. Nor had it existed in the first year of the reign of Ay, his successor, because Aaron was born at that time and did not need to be hidden from the eyes of the Egyptians.

We are not just looking for someone who crushed the slaves by his building demands. We are searching for a pharaoh whose personality fit the profile of someone who could issue a very harsh edict—demanding the death of every male Hebrew baby to cut down on the enormous Hebrew slave population—to reduce the threat this excessive population posed to Egypt's safety. This search had led us to a pharaoh whose main goal was to safeguard Egypt from repeating dark times in its history and to restore it to its former splendor. Such a pharaoh was Haremhab. However, although he fits into the general period we are studying, he does not meet the two additional requirements: having a daughter who adopted one of the condemned male Hebrew babies, Moses, as her own son,[67] and reigning in 1328 B.C., the year Moses was born.

---

66 Exodus 2:2-4

67 Exodus 2:5-10

Let's do some detective work to study the pharaohs of the XIX Dynasty and the very end of the XVIII Dynasty, including the dates they reigned and other pertinent historical details. We will search for the pharaoh who issued the harsh edict, reigned the year Moses was born, and who had a daughter who adopted a condemned male Hebrew baby.

To provide a clearer visual idea of the family relationships that will be described in the following pages, I've inserted a genealogical chart, Chart 5. Please—refer to the chart as often as necessary.

Chart 5
A Royal Genealogy of the XVIII Dynasty

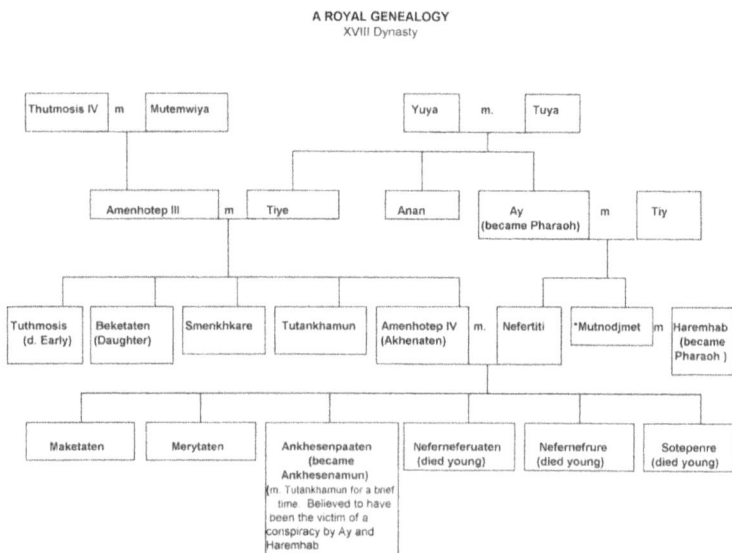

A ROYAL GENEALOGY
XVIII Dynasty

Pharaoh Ay reigned after Tutankhamun and was on the throne when Moses was born in 1328 BC. Ay was king for only four years, from 1331 BC to 1327 BC. He was a commoner who lived during the reign of Tuthmosis IV. His father was named Yuya, and he served in the position of Master of the Horse; his mother was named Tuya and she served as high priestess. Ay had a brother, Anen, who held high offices in the priesthood; he had a sister, Tiye, who married Tuthmosis IV's son, Amenhotep III. Under the latter's reign, Ay held the post of Chariot Commander and, eventually, inherited all the offices which his father, Yuya, had held, and was appointed King's Deputy.

Ay was married to a fellow commoner named Tiy and had two daughters—the beautiful and well-known Nefertiti and her lesser-known sister Mutnodjmet. Please refer to Chart 5 to clarify their positions in relation to one another.

Amenhotep III, Ay's brother-in-law, had four sons: the eldest, Thutmosis, who must have died early; the next, Amenhotep IV, later known as Akhenaten, the heretic king; followed by Smenkhkare and Tutankhamun; he also had a daughter, Beketaten. After Amenhotep III's death, Akhenaten succeeded his father to the throne.

Akhenaten married Nefertiti, his cousin, the elder daughter of his uncle, Ay, and had six daughters, but nothing is known of the fate of the last three.[68] Upon Nefertiti's

---

68 Cyril Adred, *Akhenaten And Nefertiti*, (New York: The Viking Press, Inc., 1973), p. 20.

death, he married his eldest daughter, Merytaten, and the next, Maketaten, and so on down the line. When his brother, Smenkhkare, reached manhood at sixteen, he married Akhenaten's eldest surviving daughter, Ankhesenamun (also known as Ankhesenpaaten) and was made co-regent at the same time. After he ascended the throne, Akhenaten denied the worship of the Egyptian god Amun, along with all the other gods. His daughter's name ending was changed to indicate her father's establishment of the god Aten, the sun disk, as the only god to be worshiped.

Before all these names, marriages, and relationships become too confusing, we need to divert our attention to another subject: Egyptian marriage customs that led to attaining the throne by legal means. Learning about these customs will help us understand how two commoners could have become kings of Egypt. In Chapter VII, we will continue our search for the pharaoh of the oppression, whose edict sought the death of all male Hebrew babies, after we take this "detour" in Chapter VI.

Chapter VI

UNDERSTANDING EGYPTIAN MARRIAGE CUSTOMS
MATRILINEAL ROYAL DESCENT

The legitimate right to the throne, as well as to the inheritance, was carried through the female line. The king's first wife was called the "Great Wife," or chief queen; she was considered the wife of a god. If her own father had previously been a pharaoh, she was thought to have within her "some of the divine being."[69] The eldest daughter of the chief queen carried the succession handed down by her mother, and her eldest daughter was the Great Wife of the next generation.[70] This custom is called matrilineal descent.

For a male aspirant to the throne to realize his goal, he had to marry the royal heiress; this guaranteed his accession unless a divorce or death of the heiress ensued. In the case of divorce, the woman retained all rights as heiress,

---

69 John A. Wilson, *The Culture Of Ancient Egypt*, rev. ed. (1959; Chicago: The University of Chicago Press, 1963, p. 96.

70 Warner A. Hutchinson, *Ancient Egypt, Three Thousand Years of Splendor*, (New York: Grosset & Dunlap, 1978), pp. 96, 97.

which, upon her death, passed on to her daughters—or, if she had none, to her sisters. In the case of Nefertiti, her daughters inherited the right to the succession. However, since all of them and their offspring died, the right to the throne went to Nefertiti's sister, Mutnodjmet.

> "The old matriarchal principle that property descended in the female line, from mother to daughter, still held well, and the husband enjoyed his wife's inheritance only while the marriage lasted. If she were divorced she kept it, and if she died it passed to her daughter."[71]

In the royal family, marriages of brothers to sisters, fathers to daughters, and mothers to sons were freely accepted by the Egyptians. Blood relationships did not matter. These intra familial marriages were an effort to preserve the purity of the royal lines, although, occasionally, as we have seen, commoners' blood was intermingled. Since polygamy was customary among the ruling classes, the man often married the immediate heiress as well as several sisters or daughters who were next in the line of succession. They were considered queens, with the first one being the "Great Queen." Their firstborn sons were candidates for the throne, provided they married the appropriate heiress.

"It...becomes evident that a pharaoh safeguarded

---

71 R.R. Sellman, op.cit., p. 54.

---

himself from abdication by marrying every heiress without any regard to consanguinity, so that if the chief heiress died, he was already married to the next in succession and thus retained the sovereignty...the throne went strictly in the female line. The Great Wife of the king was the heiress; by right of marriage with her, the king came to the throne. The king's birth was not important, he might be of any rank, but if he married the queen he at once became king. To put the matter in a few words: the queen was queen by right of birth, the king was king by right of marriage."[72]

Ramses II is a good example of this: he married his mother, Tuya, and all her daughters (who were also his daughters as well as his sisters), thus ensuring his position as Pharaoh.[73] Even a man of non-royal blood could become king by marrying the previous king's widow, her sister (if she was the heiress), or the former king's daughter or her sister.[74]

Returning to Ay, the commoner married to a commoner, Tiy—how did he become Pharaoh? After

72 Leonard Cottrell, *Life Under The Pharaohs*, (New York: Holt, Rineheart and Winston, 1960), pp.91, 92.

73 Margaret Alice Murray, *The Splendor That Was Egypt*, rev. ed. (1949; New York: Hawthorn Books, Inc. Publishers, 1969), p. 102.

74 Lisa K. Sabbahy, *Ramses II: The Pharaoh And His Time*, (Provo, Utah: Brigham Young University Print Services, 1985), p. 6.

Tutankhamun's death, he married the latter's widow and heiress, who also happened to be his granddaughter, Ankhesenamun. When she died, he married his own daughter, Mutnodjmet, the sister of Queen Nefertiti and only surviving heiress, as will be discussed further. Thus, Ay guaranteed he would become Pharaoh after Tutankhamun's death.

We have been considering the importance of maintaining the purity of the royal lines, one of the purposes of matrilineal descent. However, there is an exception to this rule found in Amenhotep III's wife, who was a commoner:

> "At the beginning of his reign Amenhotep III was already married to a woman named Tiy, the daughter of a commoner by the name of Yuya and his wife Tuya. In spite of her humble origin, Tiy was elevated to the rank of 'Great Royal Wife,' which established her as queen consort."[75]

It should be clearer now why, upon Nefertiti's death, Akhenaten married his eldest surviving daughter, Ankhesenamun (known as Ankhesenpaaten during Akhenaten's reign, in honor of the god Aten). She had inherited the right to the throne from her mother, Nefertiti, and from her elder sisters. Since Akhenaten wanted his brother, Smenkhkare, to be co-regent with him, he allowed the latter to marry Ankhesenamun, as well.

75 G. Steindorff and K.C. Seele, op.cit., p. 74.

Upon Akhenaten's and Smenkhkare's deaths, their brother, Tutankhamun, the boy king, ascended the throne at the age of nine. To have the right to be the next pharaoh, he had to marry his brother's widow, Ankhesenamun, Akhenaten's only surviving daughter.[76] There was another woman who was also in line to carry the succession, should Ankhesenamun die, because she was Nefertiti's sister--Mutnodjmet.

There are not too many references to Mutnodjmet after a certain point in Akhenaten's reign, perhaps because she was high priestess of Amun,[77] the former principal god. Akhenaten was determined to obliterate and replace Amun along with all the other Egyptian gods with what has been called his heretical monotheism in the worship of Aten. This explains the various changes in names during Akhenaten's reign: the "amun" and "aten" endings in the names corresponded to Amun being supplanted by Aten.

To cover possible events and secure his right to the throne, Tutankhamun might also very likely have married Mutnodjmet, Nefertiti's sister, since we see her reappear as the only surviving heiress whom Tutankhamun's successor married to ensure his claim to the throne.

Tutankhamun's reign was quite short, only nine

76 K.A. Kitchen, op.cit., p.15.

77 William MacQuitty, *Tutankhamun, The Last Journey*, 3rd ed. (n.d. rpt. New York: Crown Publishers, 1978), p.54.

years. During this time, Ay and his contemporary, a general in the army named Haremhab, had been the power behind the throne, making sure that the harm done to the Egyptian religion brought upon by the reign of Akhenaten would never occur again. These two old men seemed to have been instrumental in initiating the destruction of carvings, statues, and temples to Aten, the focus of Akhenaten's monotheistic religion, and in restoring the temples and worship of the old Egyptian gods. However, it is possible that Ay might not have been a very eager participant since he had been a faithful supporter of Akhenaten.

> "Ay was definitely Akhenaten's man, his most faithful supporter in the city of the Globe (Aten), Personal Scribe to the king, the Royal Fan-Bearer, above all 'it-neter,' 'Divine Father' or 'Father of the God (the king).' Was he perhaps Pharaoh's father-in-law? It has been suggested recently that he may have been the widowed father of Nefertiti, remarried to Tey, who would then have been the nurse, or at least the stepmother of the future queen."[78]

Upon the death of Tutankhamun, which occurred at the young age of eighteen, his widow and heiress,

---

78 Christiane Desroches-Noblecourt, *Life And Death Of A Pharaoh, Tutankhamen*, 2nd ed. (1963;rpt. New York: Little, Brown and Company, 1978), p.124.

Ankhesenamun, planned to marry a Hittite prince in order to carry on the royal line:

> "...for it is repugnant to me to take one of my servants (subjects) to husband...He who was my husband is dead and I have no son.' This servant can only have been the 'scribe of the recruits,' who had become the real dictator at the palace, Horemheb, and not, as it is generally assumed, the 'Divine Father' Ay who was a close relative of the queen's, indeed probably her grandfather...Prince Zannanza of the Hittites duly set out with his escort but Horemheb's police, 'the men and the horses of Egypt,' murdered him on the way. This led to a state of war between Egypt and the Hittites...Henceforth the few who remained true to the heretical faith could no longer count upon the possibility of a marriage between the last legitimate heiress of the XVIII Dynasty and a foreign prince...For want of a foreign prince, and repelled by the notion of a 'misalliance' in her own country, the young widow was now fated to share her sovereign's duties and privileges with a co-regent. Being a timid creature, utterly unlike her illustrious forbear Hatshepsut, Ankhesenamun chose her grandfather, the vizier Ay, to play this part. The decision was taken on the eve of the official funeral of

Tutankhamun, and the 'Divine Father' Ay, wearing the 'khepresh' and animal skin, performed the ceremony of the 'opening of the mouth and eyes' by the tomb as had been done throughout the ages by royal heirs succeeding their fathers..."[79]

Ay immediately buried Tutankhamun, because another custom that would further strengthen the right to the throne set forth: "Who buries the pharaoh becomes the next pharaoh."[80] He then married Ankhesenamun, his granddaughter, the former pharaoh's widow and heiress, assuming his position as Pharaoh. As noted earlier and as was the custom, he most likely also married Mutnodjmet, who might have been Tutankhamun's other widow, next in the line for the succession, and who was also Ay's daughter. By the time Ay's reign ended with his death four years later, Ankhesenamun had died,[81] and Mutnodjmet was the sole surviving heiress to the throne of Egypt.[82]

We have taken quite a detour into the intricacies of Egyptian royal marriage customs so that we might better understand the various relationships, as well as the

---

79 C. Desroches-Noblecourt, op.cit., pp. 275, 276.

80 K.A .Kitchen, op.cit., p.15

81 Rosalie David, Ph.D., *The Making of the Past—The Egyptian Kingdoms*, (Oxford, England: Phaidon Press Ltd., 1975), p.25

82 K.A. Kitchen, op.cit., p.15.

necessity for the heir to the throne to ensure his position. We have also examined the exceptions to the rule, showing how commoners were able to become kings and queens of Egypt. Let us now return to our search for the pharaoh of the oppression, who had the daughter to whom the Bible refers as "Pharaoh's daughter."

Chapter VII

Based on the information in the previous chapter, we can consider Ay as the possible pharaoh of the oppression since he was the only pharaoh who reigned around the time in question and had a surviving daughter—especially one old enough to have had a son, whether her own or adopted. Because Ay's daughter, Mutnodjmet, was the only surviving heiress to the throne, and indeed can be called "Pharaoh's daughter," we can assume that we might be on the right path toward our goal. However, when reading the verses in the Bible that refer to Pharaoh's daughter, we tend to believe that it was her father who issued the edict demanding the death of all male Hebrew babies.

Such a man would have had a harsh character; he would have been nationalistic, having a desire for social reform. We do not have enough information about Ay's character to assert that he could have been the one to issue harsh edicts. We do know that Akhenaten highly favored him, which may be the reason the reforms that were made to remove any trace of the Akhenaten heresy were rather slow during Ay's reign in comparison with the reign of his successor, Haremhab.

In contrast, Ay made some reforms, but he was old and only reigned for four years, sharing the last year of his reign with Haremhab as co-regent:

> "The event (Haremhab's co-regency with Ay)... was consummated by marriage with the next surviving heiress, in his case not Ankhesenamun who was dead, but Mutnodjmet, the sister of Nefertiti and daughter of Ay."[83]

Wanting to ensure that his position as co-regent would not be questioned, since he was a commoner with no ties to anyone in the royal family, he confirmed his right to share the throne by marrying the only surviving heiress, Mutnodjmet. In addition, that same year, 1327 B.C., Pharaoh Ay died, and, as was the custom, the next king, General Haremhab, buried Ay,[84] which gave him the right to claim the throne of Egypt.

Although Haremhab was in his sixties when he ascended the throne, he was full of vigor and was determined to wipe out the harm brought about by Akhenaten. He issued a series of harsh laws or edicts to reestablish law and order where there had been excess and chaos.

Is it possible that Haremhab was the pharaoh who

83 C. Aldred, op.cit., p.301.

84 K.A. Kitchen, op.cit., p.15.

issued the edict demanding the death of the male Hebrew babies? There appears to be a chronological problem with this because his ascension to the throne occurred in 1327 BC and Moses was born in 1328 BC. Since the Bible states that Moses was three months old when Pharaoh's daughter found and adopted him, it would have been impossible for Haremhab to have issued any edicts at the time of Moses's birth; only the pharaoh could do such a thing.[85] Besides this, we are told that Haremhab had no heirs[86] so we cannot attribute a daughter to him.

As stated previously, such an edict was not in effect during the first three years of Ay's reign, since Aaron, who was three years older than Moses,[87] had no difficulty living with his parents openly and without fear. However, we might recall that the edict was strictly enforced at Moses's birth because his parents did hide him for the first three months of his life.[88] This would have been during Ay's last year on the throne.

As it happens, our theory aligns with the chronology. The fact that Ay appointed Haremhab to be co-regent during the last year of his reign is the key that can unravel and solve the problem with the chronology. Let us now examine this "key" considering the co-regency.

---

85 W. Hutchinson, op. cit., p.99.

86 R.E. Freed, op. cit., p.26.

87 Exodus 7:7

88 Exodus 2:4.

To celebrate and confirm this co-regency, Haremhab married Mutnodjmet, who was in her early thirties. As mentioned, marrying Mutnodjmet ensured the legitimacy of Haremhab's claim to the throne, even if he had to share it with Ay:

> "The coronation inscription on the back of a seated dyad of himself and his queen in the Turin Museum is the most complete account of his career. It traces the steps in his progress to the throne, and indirectly implies that Ay accompanied him to Karnak to attend the Festival of Southern Opet, using the occasion to obtain the sanction of the oracle of Amun to Haremhab's induction as co-regent."[89]

The Festival of Southern Opet began in the Temple of Karnak as a procession, carrying the god Amun. It continued north to the Temple of Luxor. It was during this festival that Amun would strengthen the power of the pharaoh. Haremhab's co-regency was confirmed at this time.

The Festival of Southern Opet was celebrated in the second month of the lunar calendar, which was divided into three sections of four months each: Akhet, the time of flooding; Peret, the time of sowing; and Shemu, the time of harvest. The festival, being held in the second month of Akhet, aligns perfectly with Moses being born

---

89 Cyril Aldred, *Akhenaten King of Egypt*, 2nd ed. (1988; rpt. London: Thames and Hudson Ltd., 1991), p.301.

at the end of 1328 BC, and being three months old in the second month of the lunar new year, 1327 BC—Ay's last year on the throne.

We can point to a confirmation that the edict requiring the death of male Hebrew babies could have been in effect at this time: Haremhab, now co-regent with Ay, made stronger by the god Amun during the feast, was able to return to the palace with the authority to dictate changes toward restoring law and order in Egypt.

We don't know what the relationship between Ay and Haremhab was like at this time. We do know that Haremhab soon issued The Edict of Haremhab, in which he expressed his disgust at the way things were throughout the land. There was much corruption by state officials, which began with the reign of Akhenaten and continued during the reigns of Tutankhamun and Ay. The Edict of Haremhab, which some say was written in his own hand, outlined punishments to be imposed on those who were guilty of abuses; one such punishment was cutting off the nose, followed by exile to the northern frontier. As co-regent, it would have been plausible for Haremhab, being equal in power to Ay, to add to his edict the demand for the death of every male Hebrew baby:

> "Following Ay, Tutankhamen's general Horemheb took control, battling for what had been lost in Egypt's Asian empire and restoring order at home. Akhenaten had so ignored

internal affairs while basking in the rays of his disc that government had come to a virtual standstill. An indication of how far things had gone awry is the strong edict Horemheb issued against corrupt officials—he even imposed the death penalty on any judge found taking a bribe."[90]

The following is another example of Haremhab's harshness:

"Once established, the new pharaoh embarked upon extremely violent persecutions. In order to justify them, he published an edict, known as the 'Edict of Horemheb'...The king, whose main concern was to establish law and improve the lot of his people undertook to punish all injustice and to order immediate castigations: prevaricators were to have their noses cut off and exile was reinstated as a sentence...At Thebes, too, he showed his destructiveness...With such evidence of Horemheb's ruthlessness it is not difficult to believe, as some do, that he was capable of assisting in the disposal of Ay and Ankhesenamun. Everything seems to have been methodically planned and coordinated by Horemheb...who, to woo the leaders of the counter-reformation, resorted to a type of fanaticism which has been

90   L.K. Sabbahy, op.cit., p.8.

responsible for so many crimes."[91]

The slave population had increased exponentially as the many years of slavery went by. During this time, the slaves far outnumbered the Egyptian population. As a former army general, Haremhab must have considered the danger posed by a slave population that outnumbered the Egyptians: If the slaves ever revolted, they could defeat the Egyptians, creating a scenario similar to the one that existed during the foreign Hyksos's takeover—their rule lasted one hundred and fifty-years! Doing something to keep the Hebrew numbers from continuing to grow would have been a good idea. What better way to do this than by ordering the death of every male Hebrew baby born? Haremhab's strategy, if successful, would certainly have put an end to the next generation of Hebrews, thus stunting Egypt's population growth.

Haremhab was instrumental in proposing ideas and edicts, while possessing the authority to carry these out even during the time that Ay was still on the throne:

> "The law was not codified and written law until the XXIV Dynasty. The law which was dispensed by the vizier was...phrased as the commanding word of pharaoh and arising out of pharaoh's three divine qualities of Hu, Sia and Ma'at, Authority, Perception and Justice...In Egypt, the law was personally derived from the god-king

91 C. Desroches-Noblecourt, op.cit., pp.284-285

and was tailored as justice and equity to the individual appellant."[92]

Another source states:

"In administering the government, the pharaoh was guided by the ideal of ma'at, the primary Egyptian concept of justice, which was a combination of order, truth and justice. This principle was embodied in the person of the pharaoh: he was guided by Ma'at and what he decided became ma'at."[93]

The above quotes show that the king possessed the absolute right to create any law; therefore, as co-regent, Haremhab would have shared in this "divine" right, making it entirely possible for him to have issued the harsh edict in question.

It would be wonderful if we could say that such a law was mentioned in The Edict of Haremhab. Unfortunately, this edict, found in fragments on the back of the northern Pylon X in the Temple of Karnak, did not mention deaths of the male Hebrew babies. The remains of the edict are in ruins, and only a total of about two-thirds of the carved stela remains. However, considering that Haremhab diligently set out to change the way things had been in Egypt almost as soon as his co-regency began, it is likely that

---

92 J.A. Wilson, op. cit., pp. 172, 173.

93 W. Hutchinson, op. cit., p.99

he might have ordered the death of all male Hebrew babies, a move that would certainly have reduced the future Hebrew population, thus preventing or sharply reducing future attempts at uprisings.

According to several Egyptologists, Haremhab was a man driven by the desire to restore Egypt to her former splendor. The reign of Akhenaten (under whom Haremhab had been an army general) had caused chaos in the once peaceful and orderly Egypt. Akhenaten had removed all gods except Aten, and he made worship of the latter exclusive. His reign was a time of corruption among government officials. Foreign and domestic affairs suffered because Akhenaten was more interested in the worship of his god, Aten, and in a new and revolutionary style of art, known as "the Amarna age." His focus was also on his immediate family, more than on the affairs of state. His successors and brothers, Smenkhkare and Tutankhamun, did not reign long and were young and weak.

You might remember that in the time of Tutankhamun's reign, Haremhab and Ay, also an army general, were what one might call the "power behind the throne." The "boy king" was only nine years old when he ascended the throne and reigned for a brief nine years. It was a time of upheaval that had been inherited from the reign of Akhenaten. There was need for restoration to the way things were before the time of the "heretic king" during whose reign buildings and statues of the former gods had been torn down or neglected. During the reign of Tutankhamun, Haremhab, in his role as General of the Armies, would have been quite influential in beginning the work of restoring Egypt. There is a "Restoration Stela" ascribed to the reign of Tutankhamun. Twelve years later, during the fourth year of Ay's reign and the first of the co-regency with Haremhab, the stela was usurped by Haremhab, who had his name carved over Tutankhamun's. The Restoration Stela listed all the work done to restore Egypt's buildings and to bring back the worship of the former gods.

The Edict of Haremhab is purported to be "not a code of law," but rather a series of police regulations that were "much harsher in punishment than ...earlier enactments," and "the penalties seem harsh out of all proportion to the offenses."[94] Haremhab's character is described as "harsh and uncompromising."[95]

Eager to help Egypt recuperate, Haremhab ruled her with a firm hand. It was a time of peace with foreign kingdoms; he set out to restore just and effective government, even though his methods were usually excessively severe.

Haremhab still needed a large slave force to rebuild all the temples and statues that had been destroyed or badly damaged. He could be considered a large-scale

---

94 J. A. Wilson, op.cit., pp. 237, 238, 242.

95 J.E. Manchip White, op.cit., p. 175.

builder since he also had new buildings and tombs erected. Yet, having been commander in chief of the army after Akhenaten's death, he knew what a dangerous thing
it was for Egypt to be outnumbered by the slaves, most of
whom were Hebrews, a Semitic people just as the Hyksos
had been.

The Bible says that the king of Egypt instructed the
midwives to kill the male Hebrew babies as soon as they
were born. The midwives disobeyed Pharaoh, so next he
ordered that every Hebrew son born should be put to
death. Considering Haremhab's character, it is entirely
possible that, when the subtle attempt through the midwives failed, he would publicly issue such a harsh edict
toward improving the welfare of Egypt.

If, indeed, Haremhab was the pharaoh to whom
the Bible refers as having ordered the death of the male
Hebrew babies, then who was "Pharaoh's daughter?" Who
found Moses, one of the babies ordered to be put to death,
and who adopted him as her own son? It was Mutnodjmet,
daughter of Pharaoh Ay and wife of Pharaoh Haremhab.

In view of her husband's edict, this open defiance
would seem to be impossible...or was it? In addition to
this, Haremhab is known not to have had an heir to the
throne. This could disprove our theory; yet, because of
the corrupt state in which Egypt was left by the reign of
Akhenaten, Haremhab and Seti I are the two pharaohs
who are known to have enacted edicts which were much

harsher than previous ones. In fact, it is said of Seti I, "(he) has left us a decree which shows the same brusque severity as the edict of Haremhab."[96] Perhaps the key to confirming Haremhab as the pharaoh of the oppression—the one who issued the edict sentencing to death all male Hebrew babies--can be found in researching whether or not his wife, Mutnodjmet, was the daughter of Pharaoh of whom the Bible speaks, the daughter who actually adopted Moses.

---

96 J.A. Wilson, op.cit., p. 242.

Chapter VIII

PHARAOH'S DAUGHTER

As previously mentioned, Mutnodjmet was the only woman who could be called "Pharaoh's daughter" because she was the only survivor of generations of royal daughters. She was the daughter of Pharaoh Ay and the wife of his co-regent and then successor, Pharaoh Haremhab. From what we have learned of Haremhab's harsh and nationalistic character, it was entirely possible for him to have issued the edict to control the Hebrew population. He very likely would have rationalized that such a law would be in the best interest of Egypt, its implementation removing the danger of any future uprisings from the enormous slave population.

Haremhab has been described as a ruthless, cruel man. He was someone who ruled the palace like a dictator. As mentioned in Chapter VI, he was even responsible for ordering the death of Prince Zannanzaof the Mittani. The prince was going to marry Ankhesenamun to prevent Haremhab from becoming the next pharaoh through marriage to the heiress at the time. Haremhab may have ordered the disposal of Ay and Ankhesenamun as well.[97] Picturing such a man in our mind's eye, we must wonder how his wife, Mutnodjmet, could so openly and defiantly have disobeyed her husband's royal edict by saving the life of one of the condemned male Hebrew babies and adopting him, according to the Bible. Such defiance would have undermined Pharaoh's authority, something Haremhab was very determined to restore and uphold because, under Akhenaten, the king's authority had disappeared beneath a carpet of official corruption and intrigue.[98]

From all the information we have about Haremhab, we can only imagine that he would have made a public example of Mutnodjmet. He might have had the baby taken from her and might even have ordered him put to death. He might have demanded that Mutnodjmet be put to death as well, either openly or secretly. Yet, there are historical records that continue to show her as Haremhab's queen until around his fifteenth regnal year, when she was buried in a large tomb that he had built for himself.[99] No, she was not punished for disobeying her husband's edict, either by having the baby taken from her or by having harm done to her or to the baby. But how could this be possible? It does not align with what we know of Haremhab.

---

97 C. Desroches-Noblecourt, op.cit., pp. 276, 284.

98 J.A. Wilson, op.cit., p. 242.

99 C. Aldred, op.cit., p. 302.

Our research has brought us to Haremhab, though, as the most likely author of the harsh edict mentioned in the Bible, and to Mutnodjmet as "Pharaoh's daughter," who rescued the Hebrew baby, Moses, and adopted him as her own son—the future heir to the throne of Egypt. Mutnodjmet, the only surviving heiress, had married Ay, her father, when he became Pharaoh; she could have been pregnant with her father's child the year Ay and Haremhab were co-regents—the same year the latter married Mutnodjmet.

Perhaps, as we become more familiar with Mutnodjmet, we will find still another explanation. What sort of woman could she have been? Let us wander through our imagination back to the day when she and other women of the palace went down to bathe in the Nile River, as was their daily routine. Suddenly, we can almost hear them all gasping in surprise as they saw a basket floating in the river, hidden in the bulrushes, with a baby wrapped in a blanket that probably had a Hebrew design. Even if he didn't have such a blanket, the sole fact that the baby was cast adrift and was found hidden among the bulrushes would have informed everyone that this was a Hebrew baby whose parents couldn't bear to have him killed.

What course of action did Mutnodjmet take? She might have been prompted to alert Haremhab's police about the male Hebrew baby, enabling them to carry out the law and put him to death. She might have been filled with pity for the Hebrew baby. However, a third possible reaction might have been that Mutnodjmet risked disobedience to the king's law by quietly saving the baby's life and hiding him—this did not come simply from pity.

If we could learn more about Mutnodjmet's character—what sort of woman she was; what experiences had influenced her outlook on life; what her desires and fears might have been—perhaps then we could have more certainty as to which decision she might have chosen. If she decided to save the baby, did she carry a secret this heavy in her heart—a secret which, if discovered by her husband, would undoubtedly put the baby's life, and maybe her own, in danger? Let us examine the available information about Mutnodjmet, scant though it may be.

Mutnodjmet was the younger sister of the beautiful Nefertiti, who married Akhenaten. Not much is written about her; from the information we do have, however, we can form a composite picture in our minds. She can be seen in some earlier tomb reliefs at Amarna and, especially, in her father's tomb, where she is featured most prominently:

> "She is shown in those reliefs where the detail has survived as wearing her hair arranged with a side-lock in the fashion of the earlier half of the reign, and appears to be a little older than her eldest niece Meritaten."[100]

---

100 C. Aldred, op.cit., p.20.

Mutnodjmet was familiar with life in the royal palace. Although her father, Ay, was a commoner, he was related to royalty, even if in a distant manner. If we take a glance at the Royal Genealogy in Chart 5, we can see that his mother, Tuya, was the sister of Pharaoh Tuthmosis IV. The offspring of Tuya and her brother were Tiye and Pharaoh Amenhotep III who were cousins and were married to one another as well. Ay and Amenhotep III were not only cousins; they were also brothers-in-law.

In reviewing a few previously mentioned facts, Ay's daughter, Nefertiti, married Amenhotep III's son, her second cousin, Amenhotep IV. He changed his name to one more familiar to most of us—Akhenaten. Ay was his uncle as well as his father-in-law, and Mutnodjmet, Ay's daughter, was very much a part of the royal scene. However, little is known about her position in the court of Akhenaten beyond a brief mention when she and the king's daughters were young.

As previously noted, she was high priestess of Amun,[101] a fact that would have kept her from any active participation in Akhenaten's palace because he abolished the worship of Amun, as well as that of all other gods except Aten. This may be why she is not mentioned as being in the line of succession when the king and his brother, Smenkkhare, married all the heiresses. However, during Tutankhamun's reign, when the restoration of the old

---

101 W. MacQuitty, op. cit., p. 54.

gods began and the removal of any trace of the "Akhenaten heresy" was under way, we find Tutankhamun not only married to the direct heiress, Ankhesenamun, but also to Mutnodjmet,[102] the only other heiress to the throne of Egypt.

Neither she nor Ankhesenamun produced any heirs to the throne for Tutankhamun. Yet, sadly, there were the mummies of two female fetuses found in his tomb; "one may have been five months in gestation, and the other may have died in childbirth."[103]

We have seen how Ay and Haremhab were the power behind Tutankhamun's reign; how Ay only reigned for four years, a portion of which he shared with his co-regent, Haremhab; how Ankhesenamun may have been killed by Haremhab's men within those four years, thus leaving Mutnodjmet as the sole heiress to the throne; and how Haremhab married Mutnodjmet. Two sources confirm the fact that she was not young when her marriage to Haremhab took place:

"To clinch matters Horemheb married Nefertiti's sister, Mutnedjmet who, though advanced in years, was high priestess of Amun and this was quite sufficient to legalize the succession."[104]

The other source states:

102 J. Breasted, op. cit., p. 401.

103 C. Anker, K.C. Danforth, R. Somerville, op.cit., p. 156.

104 W. MacQuitty, op.cit., p.54.

"...Haremhab proceeded to the palace and was joined in marriage to the princess Mutnezmet (Mutnodjmet), the sister of Ikhnaton's (Akhenaton's) queen, Nefer-nefru-aton (Nefertiti). Although she was advanced in years, she was 'Divine Consort,' or high priestess of Amon and a princess of the royal line, and that was sufficient to make Haremhab's accession quite legal."[105]

This information tells us that Mutnodjmet was not young, according to the way Egyptians perceived youth in the palace. She was in her early thirties when she married Haremhab. As has been previously noted, the members of the royal family married young. Ankhesenamun married Tutankhamun when she was a teenager and he was nine. Like Ankhesenamun, Mutnodjmet, too, bore him no heirs. Both women had also been married to Ay—Mutnodjmet's father and Ankhesenamun's grandfather, as was the custom in the royal palace, so he could secure the right to the throne since both were heiresses. Neither one of his two wives had borne him any heirs either.

Can we imagine a natural desperation in Mutnodjmet's motherly instinct—a strong desire to have a baby? Can we also imagine a very great pressure to bear the next heir to the throne, or a daughter to carry on the matrilineal descent, which would otherwise end with her? As a woman said to be "advanced in years" when she married

105 J. Breasted, op.cit., p. 401.

Haremhab, who himself was twice her age, we can only imagine that such a desire and pressure to bear a child would have grown in intensity as the years passed. At this point, we can only speculate; if we are going to continue to search for facts, however, we cannot let our imagination build a scenario that would make Mutnodjmet respond in any specific way when finding the male Hebrew baby. Instead, we must continue to look for information to substantiate our claims. Fortunately, we do not have to search further because archaeology and modern science have provided us with the facts we need:

> "An examination of one of the burials revealed clues that indicated it might be that of Mutnodjme, the second wife of Horemheb and probably the sister of Nefertiti. The remains were those of a woman in her forties who had had numerous pregnancies. Since we know that Horemheb died without an heir, we can only presume that his and Mutnodjme's children must have been miscarried or died in infancy."[106]

With this information, we can now flesh out our imaginary Mutnodjmet, attributing to her, according to her culture, an "advanced age" in the thirties, and the experience of several pregnancies, yet no children. This alone would give her a motive to rescue the Hebrew baby and make him her own. Any woman who has experienced the

---

106 C. Hobson, op.cit., p. 114.

sorrow of losing one baby can imagine the tremendous grief over losing many, and the longing to keep trying to have one that might live. Because of modern science and the Egyptian's beliefs and their expert practice of mummification, Mutnodjmet's mummy can silently speak to us today.

> "Mute witnesses to their times, mummies nevertheless have stories to tell about life in ancient Egypt, stories that scientists studying them extract from their bones and flesh through use of various modern medical techniques including CT scans, X-rays and forensic autopsies. Specialists have even been able to reconstitute blood cells and use them to trace kinship...The skeletal remains of 18th-Dynasty Queen Mutnodjmet turned up with those of a baby, suggesting that she died in childbirth at age 42, a dozen years after marrying Pharaoh Horemheb, a commoner who had taken the throne. The physical anthropologist studying her bones found extensive trauma to her pelvis, indicative of multiple births. But since records reveal Horemheb had no heir, her babies must have been born dead or died shortly after delivery. The scientist theorized that during her marriage Mutnodjmet may have been pregnant 13 times, and that as a result of her frustrated

efforts to bear a prince before menopause, she grew progressively anemic, until her last pregnancy claimed her life. Had Mutnodjmet given birth to a living son history might have been different. If, as some think, she was the sister of Queen Nefertiti, her offspring would have added a legitimacy to Horemheb's reign, and the 18th Dynasty, one of Egypt's most glorious, would have continued. Instead, it came to an abrupt end with Horemheb's death around 1310 B.C."[107]

It is amazing what scientific advances can tell us about people who have been dead for more than three thousand years. They have provided us with a picture of Mutnodjmet that is as clear as if we were viewing her life on a movie screen. She was about forty-two years old when she died; she had been pregnant about thirteen times, having lost all her babies either before term or after childbirth; and the thirteenth pregnancy took her life. Let us see how we can fit this information in with the facts about Mutnodjmet that we have gathered thus far.

We know that Mutnodjmet died in the fifteenth or sixteenth year of Haremhab's reign, which began with his co-regency with Ay in 1327 BC,[108] the year of Haremhab's accession to the throne. At that time, Mutnodjmet would have been in her early thirties. According to

---

107 C. Anker, K.C. Danforth, R. Somerville, op.cit., p.105.

108 K.A. Kitchen, op.cit., p.238.

marriages in the palace at that time, this would have been regarded as being "advanced in years," considering that Ankhesenamun married Smenkhkare when she was eleven or twelve years old, and fifteen or sixteen when she married Tutankhamun—who was then only nine himself. As we have established, Moses was born in 1328 BC, when Mutnodjmet was about twenty-seven years old. She had already been married to Tutankhamun, with whom she had not had any living children; perhaps, even the two mummified fetuses in his tomb might have been hers. She also had been married to her father, Ay, for a short time, but no heirs were produced with him, either.

We do not know how many of the thirteen pregnancies, which ended prematurely or at birth, had occurred before she spotted the basket in the river carrying the male Hebrew baby. However, based on what we know about Mutnodjmet thus far, it would not be too presumptuous to speculate that her heart might have skipped a beat; that a smile might have formed on her face; that a ray of hope might have dawned on her despairing maternal instincts. In such a case, it would appear to be more probable that she would have concealed the truth about where she found the baby and, especially, about his Hebrew origin, desiring to make him her own.

How easy would it have been for Mutnodjmet to keep a fictitious pregnancy and birth from her husband for twelve months, including Moses's three months of age when she found him? We might say that, under normal circumstances, it would not have been easy at all. However, having lost many babies before, it would have been natural not to want to publish any news about the expected baby until after the birth and survival were certain.

Truthfully, life in the palace at that time could not be called "normal circumstances" if we were to judge it by our present cultural standards. Egyptian royal customs would help make this possible because, in the palace, the queen lived in separate quarters from the king's.[109] And the times would make it possible because Haremhab, who was in his sixties when he ascended the throne, was busy with affairs of state of enormous magnitude:

> "His (Haremhab's) accession fell at a time when all his powers and all his great ability were necessarily employed exclusively in reorganizing the kingdom after the long period of unparalleled laxity which preceded him. He performed his task with a strength and skill not less than were required for great conquest abroad... Although a soldier, with all the qualities which that calling implies in the early east, yet when he became king he could truly say: 'Behold, his majesty spent the whole time seeking the welfare of Egypt.'"[110]

109 R.A. David, Ph.D., op.cit., p.111.

110 J. Breasted, op.cit., p.407.

Haremhab was involved in making and enforcing new laws that would right problems which arose from the official corruption during the reign of Akhenaten; he would remove all traces of that reign and of the worship of Aten. He was also involved in tremendous new building projects and in restoring or usurping old ones, replacing the original names with his own. This is what pharaohs did, influenced not always by dishonesty, but by their religious belief in the power of the spoken, written, or carved word. Such dedication to his role as pharaoh in restoring Egypt to the former ways would have taken much of Haremhab's time, energy, and attention.

If he occasionally directed his interest to his wife, Mutnodjmet, and found her pregnant or having lost yet another baby, it would not have been an unfamiliar discovery. If he suddenly found that Mutnodjmet had successfully given birth and now had a three-month-old infant, it should have been an occasion for much rejoicing in the prospect of finally being able to leave an heir to the throne of Egypt. However, there was no guarantee that Mutnodjmet's baby would not die in infancy as did all the others. Perhaps, in a jaded way, Haremhab might not have had any interest in an infant until he was sure that the child would survive beyond his early years.

Usually, the king would not be interested in his children, even in the crown prince, until the latter finished his education under a tutor and his training as high priest of Amun, when the crown prince would be about twenty years old. At roughly that age, the pharaoh would take his son with him to experience battle, although in a protected manner.

The Bible tells us that Pharaoh's daughter drew the baby out of the water and named him Moses.[111] The name means "bring or take out, remove, extract" from a Semitic root; in Egyptian, it means "boy son."[112]

The Bible also tells us that Moses's sister, Miriam, kept a watchful eye on her brother while he floated among the bulrushes.[113] Additionally, it states that, when Pharaoh's daughter took him from the river, Miriam offered her own mother (who was Moses's real mother, too), as wet nurse, which Pharaoh's daughter accepted.[114] Although all of this may seem strange in our culture, the Bible accurately describes the way these things were done in Ancient Egypt. The fact that Pharaoh's daughter, Mutnodjmet, named Moses, whom she adopted as her own "boy son," is in keeping with custom:

> "At birth the child was given a name by its mother. The choice of name was motivated by one of several factors. Some names reflected the immediate circumstances of the birth..."[115]

---

111 Exodus 2:10.

112 W. Keller, op.cit.15.

113 Exodus 2:4.

114 Exodus 2:7-9.

115 Miriam Stead, *Egyptian Life*, (Cambridge, Massachusetts: Har-

Mutnodjmet appeared to name Moses after the immediate circumstances surrounding his "birth," which, for
her, was when she drew him out of the river.

In households other than the palace, the mother took
care of the children for the first three or four years, with
them being breastfed by her for the first three:

> "The mother had the charge of the child during
> its infancy; she nursed it for three years and car-
> ried it on her neck."[116]

In the royal household, "nurses" often assumed the
responsibility of nursing the child and taking the place
of the mother:

> "The queen's household was also numerous, and
> included nurses and tutors for the princes and
> princesses, keepers of the apartments, keepers of
> the wardrobe, etc."[117]

The nurses frequently took on great importance in
the life of the princes or princesses in the palace, while
the queens "did not take their duties quite so serious-
ly."[118] This helps us understand why Mutnodjmet would
have been happy to have Moses's mother be his nurse for

---

vard University Press, 1986), p. 20.

116 A. Erman, op.cit., p.163.

117 E.A. Wallis Budge, *The Dwellers On The Nile*, rev. ed. (1926; rpt.
New York: Dover Publications, Inc., 1977), p. 90.

118 P. Montet, op.cit., p.60.

the first three or four years of his life, raising him in the queen's quarters of the palace. It also makes it easier to understand how Haremhab would not have suspected that anything was out of the ordinary if he did not have close contact with the baby, whom he could easily believe was his own. All the details depicted for us in the Bible thus far are in complete accordance with the Egyptian historical records. Pharaoh's daughter finding Moses, rescuing him, adopting him as her own son, naming him, and having him brought up in the palace as the next heir to the throne of Egypt are all distinct possibilities, according to life in the Egyptian palace.

There is another possibility that would make Pharaoh's daughter and Haremhab's wife, Mutnodjmet, perfectly within her right to openly adopt the male Hebrew baby she found in a reed basket floating in the water: the Egyptian view of adoption. There is an Adoption Papyrus, but it was not recorded until a later time. Before that document, adoption agreements occurred verbally; the spoken word was believed to have magical power.

One of the main responsibilities for an Egyptian queen was to provide an heir who would continue the succession to the throne. The XVIII Dynasty would come to an end if Haremhab and Mutnodjmet had no heirs. If the Dynasty ended, the heir to the throne would have to come from a different bloodline; this is what eventually happened.

It was perfectly acceptable to select a person to be "adopted" and carry on the inheritance to the next generation. In non-royal households, sometimes the person adopted could be an adult, even one's wife, if there was no offspring. Both the husband and wife would enter into an agreement that the husband's property would belong to the wife following his death. Sometimes, a person other than the couple would be "adopted" so that, in exchange for the inheritance, he or she would provide care upon their death and even into the afterlife. There were instances when a wife could be adopted by her husband, indicating his wish that she pass the inheritance to an heir if she remarried after his death. In all cases of adoption, the goal was to preserve and hand down the inheritance when there was no heir.

In the case of the royal household, the inheritance being passed down was of great importance to the welfare of Egypt: it would provide a king to rule, maintain stability, and protect the land. It would also maintain the succession, thus preserving the Dynasty.

This way of looking at adoption is very well in keeping with Mutnodjmet—who as Pharaoh Ay's daughter and Haremhab's wife had had no living heirs. It would have been acceptable to everyone, including Haremhab, for her to adopt the baby she had found and proclaim him the next heir to the throne, thus continuing the Dynasty.

Yet, if Moses was raised in the palace and groomed to

be the next pharaoh, as the Bible clearly states, then why is it that we do not find him in the list of kings of Egypt? Why is not even the fact that he was raised as a crown prince mentioned in any historical documents, monuments, or inscriptions? Why is Haremhab recorded, in everything written about him, as having died without an heir? And one final question: Why did the XVIII Dynasty come to an end, which reinforced the fact that there was no heir to inherit the throne?

Has all our research up to this point steered us in the wrong direction—led us to the wrong conclusions? Come with me as we search for answers to these questions, seeking to fill the "Moses gap" that exists in the historical records.

Chapter IX

All the research we have done thus far has shown us that the biblical and historical accounts appear to agree—if not in the black and white written pages, at least in the spaces between the lines. We find this agreement not in what the Egyptians directly recorded, but in what they told us indirectly, as part of writings on other subjects. Nevertheless, we seem to have reached an obstacle.

We can find agreement as to the assumption that Moses would have been raised in the palace during his first three years; later, we will find further agreement as we discuss his training as a prince. However, we cannot find an opening in the list of kings for him to have become the next pharaoh. A new dynasty and other pharaohs continue the succession as if Moses was not considered at all.

We agreed that Haremhab's successor, Ramses I, was a logical choice in view of Moses's young age. Yet, by the time Pramesses became Ramses I, Moses was thirty-three years old and mature enough to have taken his place as the rightful heir to the throne. If respect for Haremhab's choice for a successor prevented Moses from forcing himself onto the throne, he should have been considered as co-regent in order to be able to claim the right to become the next pharaoh. However, Haremhab chose Ramses I instead of the man who had been raised for the throne from infancy—Moses, the legitimate heir, the "son" of the last heiress, Mutnodjmet.

Since there was no other heiress to take her place in the succession, twenty years after Mutnodjmet's death, a year after ascending the throne, Ramses I found no obstacle in the way of making his son, Seti co-regent. Guided by paternal instinct, perhaps Ramses I wanted to ensure that his own son would be the next king. Ramses I reigned for less than two years, with Seti by his side for most of that time. Upon his death, Seti buried his father, thus making his claim to the throne legal. No dispute seems to have arisen about his right to become king.

From all of this, we can gain some insight into the character of Moses and of Seti I. As depicted in the Bible, throughout his later years, Moses seems to have been a humble man; such a character trait would account for his not having fought for his right to be the next king of Egypt.

We know of no objections raised by Moses when Seti's accession to the throne occurred. He could have easily protested this on the grounds that he was the only legitimate heir according to matrilineal descent, and that he had been groomed for the throne from childhood. He also did not step in to bury Ramses I, a deed that would have further sealed his right to the throne. He seems to have silently stepped aside, allowing Seti to become king of Egypt.

When Seti I became Pharaoh, his son, Ramses, was ten years old. Perhaps for the same reasons that Pharaoh Ay and Pharaoh Haremhab did not want to have a child on the throne again, Seti did not name Ramses Crown Prince. In fact, the latter never held that title, although years later, as Ramses II, he gave elaborate details about his father appointing him to that position.[119] Actually, Seti, who was also a military man, as his father and Haremhab had been, put the welfare of Egypt first, as did the two former pharaohs. He, too, was zealous to get Egypt back on its feet as a strong empire. As one of the warrior pharaohs, he spent much time in battle to regain lands lost during the Akhenaten years.

Clearly, Seti was a man who did not let his ambition for his own son get in the way of making a wise decision for the future of the Egyptian throne. Moses was thirty-four years old a year older than Seti himself, when Seti became the new pharaoh. What could have been a better choice for Seti's successor than the man who, from childhood, had been groomed to be king, beginning under the reign of Haremhab? He may even have been regarded as

---

119 J. Breasted, op.cit., pp. 419, 420.

Haremhab's son at one time since Mutnodjmet was his mother—albeit his adoptive mother. After Seti's death, Moses would have been mature enough to step into his place as successor to the throne and carry on in the manner of Haremhab, Ramses I, and Seti I, putting the welfare of Egypt before all else. And, because Moses was already the crown prince by right, Seti would have continued to refer to him as such—a reason why later Egyptologists might have assumed Seti had an elder son who was the Crown Prince.

There are historical documents in which we can find an amazing bit of information revealing that, although he was not featured by name, Moses's presence as Crown Prince during the reign of Seti I is indeed referenced. In these documents, there is mention of a crown prince whose name is unknown, who is assumed to be a son of Seti I, and an elder brother of Ramses II. There is mention of one whose existence has been obliterated from wall carvings, paintings, and monuments, in the typical Egyptian manner that was used whenever rulers wished to change the past:

> "As the thirtieth anniversary of his nomination as crown prince approached, Seti began the preparation of the necessary obelisks; and about the same time his eldest son whose name is unknown to us, was appointed to the succession as crown prince. Desirous of appearing to have

shared in the achievements of his father, this prince had his figure inserted in the scene on the north wall of his father's Karnak Hall, showing him in battle with the Libyans. As his figure is not original here, there was not room for it and part of an inscription had to be chiseled out in order to create the necessary space. The fraud is visible to this day, the colour by which it was once disguised having now vanished."[120]

Fig. 2
Image from James Breasted's **A History of Egypt**

The above photograph (Fig. 2) was taken at the north wall of the Temple of Karnak, where there are several images depicting Seti I in battle. It is placed here to give a bigger picture of that section of the wall reliefs. The area at the top, right side of the photograph can be seen more

120 J. Breasted, op.cit., p.419

clearly in the next photo (Fig. 3), taken from G. Maspero's book,[121] which is identical to Breasted's photograph, except that the details can be seen much more clearly.

Fig. 3
Image from G. Maspero's **History of Egypt, Vol. V of XIII**

The photograph above (Fig. 3) is really two battle scenes. To the left, holding a Libyan's arm and poised to kill him, is Seti I. To the right is Seti I leading his chariot. Behind the wheel of the chariot, there is an area that has been altered. The original figure was gouged out, and another figure has been put in its place. As for the battle scene on the left, drawings have been made to clarify the area behind Seti's right foot. The following image (Fig.4) is a drawing of that scene.

121 G. Maspero, *History of Egypt, Chaldea, Syria, Babylonia and Assyria*, trans. M.L. McClure (London: The Grolier Society Publishers, n.d.) Vol. V, p. 163).

Fig. 4
Image from
James Breasted's
A History of
Egypt

The drawing above (Fig. 4) is a close-up of the area behind Seti's right foot, which makes the double image clearer. In an even closer drawing (Fig. 5) of the same area, notice the two sets of feet going in opposite directions. There are two people where there should have been one—the Crown Prince.

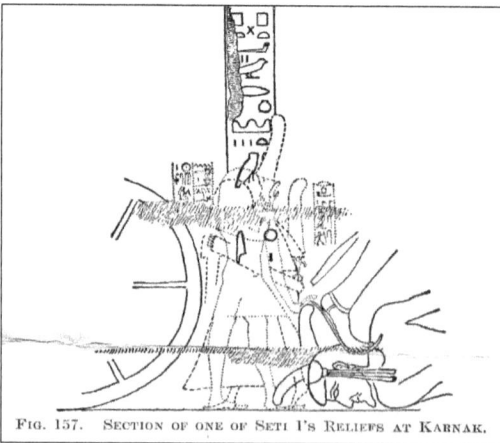

FIG. 157.   SECTION OF ONE OF SETI I'S RELIEFS AT KARNAK.

Fig. 5
Image from
James Breasted's
A History of
Egypt

"The *broken* lines(Fig. 5) are the figure of Seti's first

born son, who had himself inserted here long after the completion of the reliefs, so that a column of the original inscription now continues down into the figure. The 'dotted' lines show the form of Ramses II, inserted by him over that of his elder brother whom he displaced and supplanted."[122]

James Breasted goes on to say:

"Ramses, another son of Seti, born to him by one of his queens named Tuya, was however, plotting to supplant his eldest brother, and during their father's last days Ramses laid his plans so effectively that he was ready for a successful coup at the old king's death. Some time before the approaching jubilee, while the obelisks for it were still unfinished, Seti died, having reigned over twenty years since his own father's death...The plans of the young Ramses were immediately carried out. Whether his elder brother gained the throne long enough to have his figure inserted in his father's reliefs or whether his influence as crown prince had accomplished this, we cannot tell. In any case Ramses brushed him aside without a moment's hesitation and seized the throne. The only public evidence of his brother's claims, his figure inserted by that of Seti in the battle with the Libyans...was

122 J. Breasted, op.cit., p.419.

immediately erased with the inscriptions which stated his name and titles; while in their stead the artists of Ramses inserted the figure of their new lord, with the title 'crown prince,' which he had never borne. The colour which once carefully veiled all traces of these alterations has now long since disappeared, and the evidence of the bitter conflict of the two princes involving of course the harem and the officials of the court and a whole lost romance of court intrigue may still be traced by the trained eye on the north wall of the Karnak hypostyle."[123]

There is further evidence of this crown prince in a drawing found in Steindorff's and Seele's book (Fig. 6) that was based on a wall relief in the temple of Karnak depicting Seti I returning from a Syrian campaign. Behind the wheels of the king's chariot, the place where the crown prince was always shown, a figure appears to have been gouged out and another carved over it it.[124]

All these reliefs and drawings show a missing figure, an "elder son," a crown prince, with another carved over it. Let us remember that Ramses was only ten years old during the Libyan and Syrian campaigns, which occurred in the first year of Seti I's reign. At that time, Moses was thirty-four years old.

123 J. Breasted, op.cit., pp. 418, 419.

124 G. Steindorff and K.C. Seele, op.cit., p. 249

Fig. 6 - "Return of Sethi I from a Syrian Campaign (Karnak)"
Image from General Research Division, The New York Public
Library. "Thèbes, Karnac [Thebes, Karnak]. Palais de Ménephtha
Premier, paroi gauche." The New York Public Library
Digital Collections. 1845.

There is no mention in any documents or carvings that this eldest son could be Moses. However, if we speculate that this crown prince and assumed-to-be son of Seti I was indeed the Moses who was raised in the palace in the manner of a crown prince,[125] as the Bible says, then we can assume that Seti I would have taken Moses into a relationship similar to that of a father and son—despite their ages being one year apart, which would have put them on a more equal standing. It is logical to think that Seti would have taken the adult Moses, rather than the child Ramses, to battle with him. In fact, another source states:

"During the fierce conquest of Canaan and Phoenicia, young prince Ramesses was firmly

125 Acts 7:21, 22.

and prudently kept at home... (*It was not until*) Prince Ramesses was nearly fourteen or fifteen years old, that he was permitted his baptism of war and victory. In the ensuing brief but sufficient campaign, he was probably not allowed too close to the firing-line, but it was a beginning. When the great battle-scenes of the war were engraved at Karnak, young Ramesses' role was so minor that he was omitted from the original design. But soon, orders were given to squeeze in his modest figure, as would-be combatant with his father against a Libyan chief."[126]

During the first and second year of Seti I's reign, we can imagine that Seti might have shared affairs of state with Moses, preparing him, as Crown Prince, to be the next king. As mentioned earlier, Ramses never held the title of "crown prince," nor was he legitimately depicted in any battle with his father.

Our speculation about Seti and Moses is entirely possible. What we are doing here is theorizing as to how Moses could have fit into the available facts that have been unquestionably recorded in paintings, carvings, and reliefs. This sort of theorizing, speculating, imagining is nothing new; Egyptologists, like Champollion, have done it ever since the Rosetta Stone unlocked the mystery of the meaning of its hieroglyphics. Ever since Carter

---

126 K.A.Kitchen, op.cit., p.24.

laid eyes on Tutankhamen's opened tomb even up to our present decade, Egyptologists have been speculating and make assumptions, although they have at their disposal the tools of the modern age—CT scans, X-rays and DNA sequencing—that are continuously making unprecedented progress. As new discoveries are made, arguments against prior discoveries arise: This is the reason there are disagreements among renowned historians about relationships, such as, "Was Tutankhamen Akhenaten's brother or son?"; "How was Smenkhare related—was he Tutankhkamen's father or brother?"; "Was Mutnodjmet Nefertiti's sister?"; "Did Seti I have a son who was crown prince, born before Ramses II?"

There are spelling discrepancies because Egyptians wrote phonetically; there are disagreements as to the assignment of dates for the beginning and end of the reign of various pharaohs because unpopular kings were obliterated from some of the Egyptian records, while archaeologists found evidence of their existence. Because of their religious beliefs that were centered on magic, ancient Egyptians thought nothing of changing their history. One example of this is the belief that when names were spoken, the dead were brought to life; likewise, names that were not spoken—or were gouged out of carvings, paintings, and history—ceased to exist.

It is possible that our theorizing might be correct in how it happened that the mysterious crown prince was, indeed, Moses. Then, we could better understand why Ramses would be jealous of his "elder brother" who had taken the place he felt rightly belonged to himself. The plot mentioned above to supplant Moses as the next pharaoh of Egypt, is perfectly logical in this light.

As indicated earlier, the biblical description of Moses's rearing in the palace as a prince and, later, as crown prince, can be substantiated by what Egyptologists have discovered about Egyptian customs. When a male child became four years old, it was time to leave his mother, and, if he was a commoner, to be under his father's supervision in his education;[127] if he was a prince, he was "entrusted to persons of high rank who had grown old in the royal service."[128] These persons became tutors to the prince in a special part of the palace, "in the home of their father." The tutor who was "one of the highest court officials, was called...their 'nurse.'"[129] In the case of the crown prince, the priests undertook his education:

> "All the Pharaohs had a priestly training, and therefore were highly educated according to the standards of the time. They were great travelers also and had considerable knowledge of other countries besides their own."[130]

---

127 A. Erman, op.cit., p. 164.

128 P. Montet, op.cit., p. 60.

129 A. Erman, op.cit., p. 77.

130 M.A. Murray, op.cit., p. 107.

The same source gives the example of the career of a high priest of Amun named Bak-en Khonsu, in his own words. It reveals that he spent four years as a child; twelve years as a youth, when, at the age of sixteen, he entered training in the temple as a libation priest, until the age of twenty. From then, he went through four stages for thirty-nine years, until he was nearly sixty. At this age, he became high priest of Amon, the highest office of all.[131] The pharaoh, without spending thirty-nine years in training, automatically became high priest of Amun just because he was "Amun incarnate."[132]

Referring to Moses, the Bible says that he was "learned in all the wisdom of the Egyptians, and was mighty in words and in deeds."[133] One of the things the crown prince had to learn during his training as high priest of Amun was a different manner of speaking when performing incantations:

> "During the ceremony of the opening of the mouth of the dead, it was all important to give him not only the words of power, but also, the ability to utter them correctly and in such wise that the gods and other beings would hearken to them and obey them."[134]

131 M.A. Murray, op.cit., p. 107

132 W. Hutchinson, op.cit., p. 97.

133 Acts 7:22.

134 E.A. Wallis Budge, *Egyptian Magic*, rev. ed. (1909; New York: Do-

Again, the same source says of Moses:

> "...there are numerous features in the life of this remarkable man (Moses) which show that he was acquainted with many of the practices of Egyptian magic. The phrase 'mighty in words' probably means that, like the goddess Isis, he was 'strong of tongue' and uttered the words of power which he knew with correct pronunciation, and halted not in his speech, and was perfect both in giving the command and in saying the word."[135]

The wisdom of the Egyptians included being "skilled in reading the stars, in interpreting omens, in casting nativities, in telling fortunes, and in predicting the future of the unborn child, and in working magic of every kind." This wisdom also meant being skilled in every aspect of religion as well as being knowledgeable in reading, writing, law, medicine,[136] and, as mentioned above, in geography, and in military strategies.

All the training that Moses received as Crown Prince at the hands of the priests of Egypt would become an asset he would be able to use later in the deliverance of the Hebrew people, as we shall see in the biblical account.

Let us go back in time once more, imagining ourselves

---

ver Publications, Inc., 1971), pp. 196, 197.

135 E.A.W. Budge, op.cit., pp. 4, 5.

136 J.E. Manchip White, op.cit., p.46

in the palace where Moses had been brought up to not only believe in the gods of the Egyptians, but to actually officiate in their worship as high priest. The only way he could have carried this out effectively would be if, while engaged in such activities, he did not know the truth about his Hebrew background. In such a scenario, neither his own mother nor Mutnodjmet could have informed him about his true origins until late in his life in the palace.

When we read the narrative about Moses in the Bible, we could not conclude that such a man could be so dishonest as to act out the worship of Egyptian gods if he did not believe in them. As Crown Prince, going to the Syrian and Libyan campaigns with Seti I, he would have betrayed his dishonesty if he were not truly convinced that he would be the next pharaoh of Egypt. We would, therefore, have to assume that such information about the fact that he was a Hebrew came soon after Seti I took him on those battles. In fact, between the fifth and seventh year of Seti I's reign, nothing more is said about the "elder brother" of Ramses. This would have been between the years 1289 and 1288 BC, and Moses would have then been thirty-nine or forty years old. From that time on, there is no mention of the existence of the crown prince. Instead, there are original carvings and reliefs that show Ramses, without any alteration, accompanying his father in battle, behind Seti's chariot.

At this time, Ramses would have been about sixteen years old, which is the appropriate time for the heir to the throne to be seen taking part in warfare along with his father.[137] In fact, almost halfway into Seti I's reign, Ramses was declared to be the Prince-regent and, accordingly, he was given a harem full of beautiful women chosen by his father. At this point, "young Ramses began his own family,"[138] as was the Egyptian custom for a prince who was appointed to rule beside his father, Pharaoh, although as Prince-regent, Ramses did not have the same authority his elder brother, the crown prince, once had. Clearly, something occurred that suddenly changed the succession to the throne of Egypt.

What could have happened that changed Seti's choice of the next ruler of Egypt? It would have been a terrible event that would cause him to obliterate the existence of his Crown Prince from every carving, relief, and painting. One would imagine that a sense of having been betrayed would compel Seti to remove Moses's name from everything, even from speech. This would align with the Egyptian belief about a person's name:

> "The writing of a man's name could perpetuate his memory; its subsequent destruction produced the contrary result."[139]

---

137 J.E. Manchip White, op.cit., p. 14.

138 R.E. Freed, op.cit., p. 29.

139 T.G.H. James, op.cit., p.133.

In other words, the removal of someone's name was the equivalent of having that person erased from the memory of all people, as if he had never existed. Names were thought to have magical powers, as were words. The Egyptians believed that each word contained creative power so that, simply by speaking a word or writing it down, they could bring something into existence. The opposite of this is also true—by not speaking a word or a name, they could destroy a person's life. They would employ this same belief when putting a curse on a person's name; they would write the names of enemies on clay tablets and, by smashing these, would exterminate the enemies. This was part of the "words and deeds" magic which was very familiar to Moses:

> "The curse was a special form of linguistic magic, which could be strengthened by means of symbolic rites..."[140]

Gouging out Moses's image and name from every carving, relief, painting, papyrus, and from speech was the equivalent of having put an end to his life. There is a XVI or XVII Dynasty decree that speaks about a priest of the Koptos Temple who was thought to have committed treason or an equally serious offense:

> "The penalty was removal from office and the expunging of his name from official records, with

140 Manfred Lurker, *The Gods And Symbols Of Ancient Egypt*, rev. ed. (1974; rpt. London: Thames and Hudson Ltd., 1984) p. 130.

the confiscation of his temple property...'Let his name not be remembered in this, as should be done to one like him, a rebel and an enemy of his god. His writings shall be removed from the Temple of Min, from the treasury, and on every document likewise.'"[141]

The silence about Moses occurred when he was forty years old, simultaneous with Ramses having taken his place as heir to the throne, around 1288 BC. This is the age[142] at which the Bible says that Moses intervened on behalf of the Hebrews, whom he considered to be his people, and killed an Egyptian:

"One day, after Moses had grown up, he went out to where his own people were and watched them at their hard labor. He saw an Egyptian beating a Hebrew, one of his own people. Glancing this way and that and seeing no one, he killed the Egyptian and hid him in the sand. The next day he went out and saw two Hebrews fighting. He asked the one in the wrong, 'Why are you hitting your fellow Hebrew?' The man said, 'Who made you a ruler and a judge over us? Are you thinking of killing me as you killed the Egyptian?' Then Moses was afraid and thought,

---

141 J.E. Manchip White, op.cit., p.242.

142 Acts 7:23.

'What I did must have become known.'"[143]

We can understand Moses's fear when he learned that his deed had been found out; no doubt its news would have reached the palace. The pharaoh was regarded as not only high priest, but also chief justice and "his slightest word was oracular."

> "In his legal capacity, the king was supposed to be accessible to all his subjects. He constituted a final court of appeal. The privilege of appeal to Pharaoh indicates his supremacy in the field of law."[144]

Homicide was thought of as a crime punishable by death, "...anyone, freeman or slave, who killed another, was punished by death."[145]

Upon hearing of Moses's criminal act, Seti I, as chief justice deciding on cases of law, would have been expected to issue an order for Moses's death. This was the man whom Seti had trusted as a son, making him Crown Prince—taking him to battle, training him in all the things necessary for Moses to succeed him to the throne. This was the man whom Seti had thought would be the best choice for the good of Egypt, above his own young son, Ramses. They had shared experiences and ideals in

143 Exodus 2:11-14

144 J.E. Manchip White, op.cit., p.16.

145 Jacques Champollion, *The World Of The Egyptians*, trans. Joel Rosenthal (n.d.; rpt. Geneva: Minerva, 1971), p.13.

the court of Haremhab and, later, in Ramses I's court. Moses had served and worshiped Egyptian gods and had been loyal to Egyptian kings. Seti must have felt deceived and betrayed by one he had trusted so much, who now professed allegiance to the God of the Hebrew slaves— and claimed to be one of them. This man, Moses, had now even killed an Egyptian.

We can imagine a sense of righteous anger rising in Seti I, perhaps mingled with a desire for vengeance and justice. As chief justice, he must have ordered that Moses be put to death. As high priest, he must have ordered the removal of Moses's name and image from every monument and document and from everyone's speech and memory. The Bible says:

> "When Pharaoh heard of this, he tried to kill Moses, but Moses fled from Pharaoh and went to live in Midian..."[146]

Although it is not recorded directly in the Egyptian historical annals, James Breasted's information about Ramses supplanting his elder brother does fit in at this specific time. It is not difficult to imagine the emotionally charged turmoil in the palace, the armies being ordered to find Moses and to put him to death, the fear which Moses must have felt as he escaped from Egypt. The historical records tell about the crown prince, the "elder son" of Seti I, being supplanted by Ramses, who inserted himself in

146 Exodus 2:15.

all the battle scenes and monuments that had previously contained his elder brother's name and image. Ramses
was in his mid-teen years when he became Prince-regent,
halfway into Seti's reign. According to the dates and the
age of Moses, who was forty when his name ceased to
exist in the palace, there is perfect correlation between
the Egyptian records and the biblical account. A further
record of these events exists, written by the nineteenth
century Egyptian historian, G. Maspero:

> "Seti had had several children by his wife Tuia,
> and the eldest had already reached manhood
> when his father ascended the throne, for he had
> accompanied him on his Syrian campaign. The
> young prince died, however, soon after his re-
> turn, and his right to the crown devolved on his
> younger brother, who, like his grandfather, bore
> the name of Ramses. The prince was still very
> young, but Seti did not on that account delay
> enthroning with great pomp this son who had a
> better right to the throne than himself."[147]

As noted previously, Egyptians believed that a person
could be removed from history, from memory and from
the affections by having his name gouged out of carvings,
reliefs and writings, and by never mentioning the name
again; in effect, it was as if the person had died, disappeared, or had never existed. In James Breasted's book, the

147 G. Maspero, op.cit., p. 185).

caption below the replica of Maspero's photograph reads, "Behind the chariot... is a later insertion of the crown prince's figure..."[148]

The time of the elder crown prince's disappearance or "death" coincides with Moses's escape from Egypt. The Bible states that Moses fled to Midian; this is consistent with what the actions of a fugitive would have been for breaking the law in Egypt. His life would have been required—so Moses fled.

A few questions might come to mind at this time: What caused the radical change in Moses's allegiance to Egypt? What made the High Priest of Amun, the crown prince and heir to the throne, take sides with the Hebrews? What changed his loyalty to Egypt, demonstrated in the fact that he was still considered heir to the throne of Egypt halfway into Seti I's reign?

What could have gone through Moses's mind that had caused him to kill an Egyptian? It is possible that his real mother, Jochebed,[149] might have told him the secret of his Hebrew background around this time. She may even have told him about the history of the Hebrews and their God. Perhaps she told him about his older brother, Aaron, and his sister, Miriam—the one concerned with his welfare when he was hidden in the bulrushes in the river, hidden from the Egyptians who were sent by Haremhab to kill

---

148 J. Breasted, op.cit., Fig. 152, opposite p. 420.

149 Exodus 6:20.

all Hebrew babies. She may have told him about his adoptive mother, Mutnodjmet, who rescued him. Jochebed must have told him, and he probably remembered how she raised him and nursed him until he was four years old—the age at which his education was taken over by tutors in the palace.

Moses would neither have learned from anyone at the palace about his Hebrew background, nor about what God had said about him becoming the deliverer of the slaves. Imagine what his thoughts might have been upon learning that he was a Hebrew, after spending forty years of his life believing himself to be an Egyptian—and not just an Egyptian, but the crown prince! Finding out that he was born to Hebrew parents who were under the yoke of Egypt's king as slaves must have wreaked havoc in his mind. He must have thought about all the time that he had been loyal to Egypt and its gods and its Pharaoh, Seti I. And now, knowing the truth, he must have felt that he had to act upon it.

I think we can better understand why Moses took the action of killing the Egyptian taskmaster who was abusing one of the Hebrew slaves. This action failed because it was Moses's timing instead of God's. The Bible says about him:

> "By faith Moses, when he was come to years, refused to be called son of Pharaoh's daughter, choosing rather to suffer affliction with the

people of God than to enjoy the pleasures of sin for a season...By faith he forsook Egypt not fearing the wrath of the king: for he endured, as seeing Him who is invisible."[150]

Will we be able to find even more evidence to confirm the fact that the Bible is accurate in what it says about Moses being very much a part of Egyptian history? The more facts we find to substantiate our theories, the more accurate the biblical claims can be considered.

---

150 Hebrews 11:24-27.

Chapter X

MOSES IN MIDIAN

In his flight from Egypt, Moses covered two hundred and fifty miles as the crow flies, from Goshen, in the Egyptian Nile Delta, through the Sinai Peninsula, to the land of Midian. Was it really necessary for Moses to travel such a distance? We can safely say that his goal of escaping the Egyptian army would have guided his choices. They were at his heels in rapid pursuit—to capture and kill him. We might remember that one of the things heirs to the throne had to learn was geography; travel was very much a part of "field training" on this subject. It is obvious that he knew his way around better than Pharaoh's army did; Moses was not captured or even found but remained very much alive in Midian. This became evident again forty years later, when he led the Hebrews through the familiar desert of Sinai rather than by way of the Mediterranean coast. Had they gone via that route, it would have taken only ten days;[151] however, they would have easily been captured because there were Egyptian fortified cities along the shorter route.

---

151 J. Breasted, op.cit., p. 409.

The Bible mentions that the journey "from Horeb (or Mt. Sinai) to Kadesh Barnea by the Mount Seir (Shur) road" only took eleven days (close to James Breasted's ten days' journey). Moses took the longer route because there were...

> "...fortified stations which protected the wells and cisterns distributed along the route from Tharu (the frontier fort of Egypt) through the desert of Gaza in southern Palestine..."[152]

These fortresses in existence in the time of Haremhab and still in the time of Ramses II, along with newer ones, are depicted in sculptures in the Temple of Karnak.[153] It would have been foolish for Moses to go by such fortresses, manned by Pharaoh's loyal men, since word might have reached them about Moses's fugitive status. Instead, Moses avoided the route that went by way of northern Sinai, thus evading the main military and trade routes on the way to Midian, where he settled.

To better picture Moses's travels, more information is needed about the land of Midian. This land is mentioned in the Bible, the Torah, and the Quran, and was in the northwest Arabian Peninsula. It was a strip of land running down the eastern shore to the Gulf of Aqaba, an arm of the Red Sea. There is a mountain range in northwestern Saudi Arabia called the Midianite Mountains.

---

152 J. Breasted, op.cit., p. 409.

153 *National Geographic*, December, 1982, p. 762

Midian was named after a son of Abraham and his wife, Keturah. It is a portion of modern-day Saudi Arabia and southern Jordan, including the southern part of the Sinai Peninsula.

Goshen and Midian are now generally identified with the eastern Nile Delta, specifically the Wadi Tumilat in Egypt (Goshen) and the Tabuk region in Saudi Arabia (Midian), east of the Gulf of Aqaba.

Let us refer back to the map on page iv (Fig. 1) to have a visual understanding of where Midian was situated, as well as where Goshen and the Sinai Peninsula were—areas where Moses and the Hebrews wandered after the Exodus.

To reach Midian, Moses had to cross the Sinai Peninsula, which is described as a huge triangle, measuring two hundred and sixty miles long and one hundred and fifty miles wide at the north, between the Gulf of Suez and the Gulf of Aqaba.[154] The people who inhabited this region, the Midianites, were a confederation of semi-nomadic tribes who were descendants of Abraham.[155] This would explain why Moses was accepted there after he probably shared the story of his Hebrew birth.

While living in Midian, Moses worked as a shepherd, tending sheep for a priest named Jethro. Eventually, Moses

---

154 Guy P. Duffield, *Handbook of Bible Lands*, 2nd ed. (1969; rpt. Glendale, California: Regal Division G/L Publications, 1971) p. 122.

155 Gen. 25:2

married one of Jethro's daughters and lived in his father-in-law's household for forty years.[156] One of Moses's duties as a shepherd was to lead Jethro's sheep to find new pastures to feed on once a grazing area was depleted. This was quite a common occurrence in shepherding because the terrain in that part of the world has always been rocky and arid;[157] thus we find that Moses and the sheep traveled long distances to find new pastures:

> "...he led the flock to the far side of the desert and came to Horeb, the mountain of God,"[158] in the south of the Sinai Peninsula. Mount Sinai or Mount Horeb, as it is also known, is the chief peak, whose elevation is seven thousand, five hundred and nineteen feet above sea level. It is located in a range of granite mountains. Today, it is called Jebel Musa, the 'Mountain of Moses.'"[159]

To this mountain, Mount Horeb, Moses led Jethro's flock in what can only appear as a divinely planned preparation for leading God's human flock forty years later. The Bible calls it the "mountain of God"; it is here that God eventually gave the Ten Commandments to the

---

156 Acts 7:30.

157 Howard F. Vos, *An Introduction to Bible Geography*, rev.ed. (1973; rpt. Chicago: Moody Press, 1983), p.43.

158 Exodus 3:1.

159 G. P. Duffield, op.cit., p.

Israelites through Moses.[160] Being familiar with this area, he must have often led the sheep through various places he had originally traveled on his way to Midian.

Moses was not aware that God was training him in guiding him to Midian and, more precisely, to Jethro's house. Not only was he being trained in guiding sheep through the rocky and arid land; he was also being trained to become humble. Here was the man who had occupied a prestigious position in Egypt, being considered not only as the "son" of Pharaoh Seti I, but he also held the position of Crown Prince, heir to the Egyptian throne, for which he had been groomed from birth.

As prince, Moses had servants meeting his every need. He had the privilege of accompanying Seti I into battles geared to expand the Egyptian empire. And, now in Midian, he no longer held any exalted position. As a shepherd, he only commanded sheep that belonged to another man. Besides this, he knew very well that being a shepherd was an occupation that was scorned by Egyptians. The Bible refers to Moses as a humble man; however, his humility came years later, as every ounce of pride was broken while he learned to surrender it during his forty years in Midian.

Toward the end of his sojourn in Midian, during one of Moses's excursions leading his father-in-law's sheep to Mount Horeb, suddenly God spoke to him out of a

---

160 Exodus 20:1-7.

burning bush. God gave Moses his commission as deliverer of the oppressed Hebrew slaves who were still in Egypt. The last time he had thought of himself as the deliverer of the Hebrew slaves, he had been full of pride. He saw himself as the one who should take sides against an Egyptian who was punishing a Hebrew slave. Moses took it upon himself to kill the Egyptian. The decision to defend the slave was done in his own will, apart from God's direction. It took forty years in the wilderness of Midian for Moses to become humble enough to be able to follow God's will for him.

We can only speculate about how Moses might have felt and thought at such a time. However, if we listen to Moses's own comments in response to God's commission, we might get some insight into his thoughts and feelings:

> "But Moses said to God, 'Who am I that I should go to Pharaoh and bring the Israelites out of Egypt?...Suppose I go to the Israelites and say to them, 'The God of your fathers has sent me to you,' and they ask me, 'What is His name?' Then what shall I tell them?...What if they do not believe me or listen to me and say, 'The Lord did not appear to me'?...Moses said to the Lord, 'O Lord, I have never been eloquent, neither in the past nor since You have spoken to your servant. I am slow of speech and tongue...O Lord, please

send someone else to do it.'"[161]

According to the Bible, Moses felt inadequate to carry out such a responsibility. Although God provided a solution after each one of Moses's objections, the latter was not easily convinced. The impression Moses gave was that he was afraid to go to the Hebrew people representing the God of the Hebrews, especially after his last rejected attempt to be their deliverer, forty years earlier. Besides, he had fled in fear, and no one in Egypt had heard from him since that time. Why should the Hebrews believe that their God appeared to Moses instead of appearing to one of them?

Moses's last objection does have some validity. He complained that he was not eloquent, nor had he ever been. He claimed to be slow of speech and tongue. Many Bible scholars say that Moses had a speech impediment such as a stutter. This is not at all possible. In a previous chapter, we have mentioned that the Bible describes Moses as "mighty in words and in deed." To be raised as Crown Prince, Moses had to be trained in the magic arts practiced then as part of their religion. All aspirants to the throne were trained to be high priests, an office that required mastery of the magic arts.

We may recall that one requirement of being the high priest was to invoke incantations. In doing so, aspirants had to use a flawless manner of speech since they believed

---

161 Exodus 3:11,13; 4:1,10,13

words had such power that, once an incantation was uttered, its power was released. They used a high-pitched voice when speaking the words of power so their normal speech might never be confused with their incantations. Had Moses stuttered or been hindered by any other type of speech impediment, he would not have been called "mighty in words." Therefore, we can be certain that there was a time when Moses spoke Egyptian flawlessly and fluently, having learned it in infancy in the palace.

Why is it that, forty years later, he says he is no longer able to speak perfectly? The explanation might be found in the fact that Moses was an Egyptian, born in Egypt to Hebrew parents, who gave him up to be adopted by Pharaoh's daughter and to be raised in the Egyptian palace. The Egyptian language was his native tongue, and he spoke it fluently. During the first four years of his life, he also learned Hebrew from his wet nurse, who happened to be his real mother. Children learn foreign languages with great ease; the earlier the learning, the less likely they would have any foreign accent.

I speak from experience—I was born in Buenos Aires, Argentina, and my first language was Spanish, which I spoke without any difficulty. At the age of six, my family and I moved to the United States. I was placed in the first grade in school, not knowing a single word of English. I learned English during that year, and I could speak it fluently. Fifty years later, while visiting Buenos Aires, I had difficulty speaking Spanish and was told I had an accent in what had once been my native tongue.

Imagine Moses being told by God that he was to return to Egypt and speak to the Hebrews and the Egyptians on God's behalf. It is no wonder Moses felt inadequate for such a job, as he would have been perceived to have an accent in both languages. After his early years of growing up around his Hebrew parents, sister, and brother, he would have spoken Hebrew without fault. After he was about four or five years old, his schooling was entirely at the hands of Egyptians. He probably didn't speak Hebrew again while being trained as a prince. Now, as he found himself in the presence of God at the age of eighty, having spent the past forty years learning and speaking Arabic, his third language, God called him to speak Hebrew to Hebrew people and Egyptian to Egyptians. Undoubtedly, the Hebrew language he learned as a child was one he remembered, but could not have spoken fluently since he would have spoken only Egyptian until he was forty years old. In Midian, for the next forty years, he would have spoken only Arabic.

As for speaking to Pharaoh and the people of the palace, not having conversed in Egyptian for forty years, we can safely assume that he spoke that language haltingly instead of fluently, and with an accent, as well. Both languages, Hebrew and Egyptian, would have been spoken slowly, perhaps with hesitation and without confidence, as forgotten words were searched for in the long dormant language recesses of his mind. Surely, he remembered what he had learned from the Egyptian magicians who trained him for the priesthood: One who represented a god and was the spokesman for that god had to speak flawlessly. How could he convince Pharaoh that he represented the God of the Hebrews if he spoke haltingly and with an accent? And he might have thought it necessary to speak Hebrew perfectly to convince the Hebrews that he was, indeed, their God's representative. It is no wonder that poor Moses felt inadequate in his linguistic abilities; although he knew three languages at eighty years of age, he would have spoken each of them with a foreign accent.

Perhaps another explanation for Moses's reluctance in doing what God requested of him was fear. When he left Egypt, his life was in danger. Although God told Moses that those who had sought his life had died by now,[162] particularly Seti I, he would have to face the new pharaoh, Ramses II, Seti I's son. Forty years before, Ramses had been bypassed in favor of Moses, who has been referred to as Ramses's "elder brother," and who was thought to have been Crown Prince and heir to the throne. Certainly, forty years was a long enough time to blur memory, and Ramses had only been fifteen or sixteen years old when Moses fled Egypt. Besides, Egyptians had not spoken about Moses nor spoken his name for the past forty

---

162 Exodus 4:19.

Alice I. Henry

years. The name "Moses," referring to the one who would have been their king, had been forgotten. All mention of him in statues, carvings, reliefs, paintings, writings, and speech had been removed. As indicated previously, it was an Egyptian custom to obliterate the memory of a person they wished to consider as dead—or worse, perhaps as if the person had never existed. There were no longer any traces that would remind anyone about the Moses who had been Crown Prince or even that he had once existed. It would have been as if Moses had never walked among the Egyptians.

The second forty years of Moses's life were ones that would naturally have changed his appearance into that of an old man of eighty. In addition, the aging effects of stress caused by the hardships he had endured in fleeing for his life and in living the life of a shepherd, dependent on his father-in-law, left their mark. We must also consider that there was a change in Moses's physical characteristics. When Moses left Egypt, he had a shaved head and face, which was typical of Egyptian nobility. After living in Midian, his hair and beard would have been long, as was the typical style for the Midianite men. Both his hair and beard would probably have been gray or even white by that time. Finally, in contrast to the white linen he was last seen wearing in Egypt, he now wore the colorful clothes of Midian.[163] One might say that no one would

163 W. Keller, op.cit, p.217.

have recognized Moses in his present condition; even his younger "brother," Ramses II, would not have known who he really was.

What about his name? Wouldn't everyone in Egypt know him by his name? No—that would not have been the case. In Egypt, the name Moses was as common as today's John or Mary. At any rate, if anyone thought about Moses at all, they probably assumed he had died by that time.

When we last saw Moses in Egypt, just prior to his escape, we saw a proud, self-reliant forty-year-old man who had been used to exercising the authority derived from his special royal position to accomplish his goals. At that time, he took the revelation about his Hebrew origin and God's plans for him and proceeded to carry them out in the same manner—with the authority of the crown prince. He was not accustomed to receiving orders or to obediently waiting for instructions to carry them out. In short, Moses would not rely on God's leadership and direction. For this reason, the experience in Midian served as a training ground to mold Moses's character. He had to become humble instead of proud; reliant on God instead of himself; experienced in leading over six hundred thousand people, besides women and children,[164] in the same way he had led Jethro's sheep every day for forty years. He had to become acquainted with all the nooks and crannies of the wilderness in the Sinai Peninsula, where he and the

---

164 Exodus 12:37, 38.

Hebrew people would wander for forty years. It took forty years for Moses, the proud Crown Prince, heir to the throne of Egypt, to become Moses, the humble shepherd who led someone else's sheep. This was all in preparation for Moses to become the deliverer whom God would use to lead the Hebrew slaves, God's people, out of Egypt en route to the place God had prepared for them.

Not only had Moses's physical appearance changed, but his pride, his arrogance, his authoritativeness, and his self-reliance were no longer evident. Moses had remained in Midian, living the lifestyle of a Midianite and a shepherd for forty years. It doesn't seem logical that God used this Midian experience to train Moses to become the leader of millions of Hebrews. One could hardly say that he was being prepared to free the Hebrew slaves against the skilled opposition of the entire Egyptian Empire through his shepherding. Against all human logic, this was God's perfect method for training Moses—his pride and arrogance became humility. In Egyptian culture, being a shepherd was considered being of the lowliest social standing, after children and women. His authoritativeness was replaced by obedience to those above him, such as his father-in-law. His self-reliance was obviously shaken as his response to God's calling indicates—he didn't feel qualified, and he wanted God to send someone else.

How did God solve the problem of Moses's difficulty with speaking fluently in both Hebrew and Egyptian? He appointed Aaron to be his spokesman. Aaron was fluent in Hebrew and Egyptian since he had lived his entire life in Goshen, where the Hebrew people lived; Moses had lived in Midian for the past forty years. In response to Moses's complaints about his difficulties with languages, in the Bible, God said:

> "What about your brother, Aaron the Levite? I know he can speak well. He is already on his way to meet you, and his heart will be glad when he sees you. You shall speak to him and put words in his mouth; I will help both of you speak and will teach you what to do. He will speak to the people for you, and it will be as if he were your mouth and as if you were God to him. But take this staff in your hand so you can perform miraculous signs with it."[165]

Aaron was known by his own people as well as by some of the Egyptians. His reputation had not suffered the stigma that Moses's had; this suffering led to Moses fleeing from Egypt as a criminal. Now Moses no longer found objections to God's plans for him. His humility and obedience were forged in the anvil of rough living, deprivation, and subjection to his father-in-law. He was trained and equipped for the task of leading God's flock, the Hebrew slaves, out of Egypt through the wilderness of the Sinai Peninsula.

---

165 Exodus 4:14-17.

As a brief note, to further understand why Moses was well qualified to lead the Hebrews out of Egypt, here are some thoughts from Phillip Keller's book, *A Shepherd Looks at Psalm 23.*[166] A shepherd not only led the sheep to find pastures, but he also went ahead of them, checking that no poisonous plants were growing among the patches of grass. Sheep are not smart enough to distinguish and avoid eating anything that might harm them. As a shepherd, Moses would make sure all the sheep were always following him because sheep are prone to getting distracted and to wandering.

At night, Moses would have counted all the sheep as they went into their enclosure to know whether any had strayed and fallen prey to predators. He also would have checked each one of them as they entered the sheep fold to see if any had suffered wounds inflicted by thorny bushes. If they had, Moses would have cleaned and anointed their wounds with olive oil to prevent infection. Shepherds were familiar with the sounds the sheep in their care made, recognizing their individual bleats. All this information adds a layer of intimacy and caring for the sheep in Moses's charge. His training in Midian certainly would have equipped him to be a humble, caring, and knowledgeable leader of God's people for forty years in the wilderness of Sinai.

---

166 Phillip Keller, *A Shepherd Looks at Psalm 23* (Zondervan, 1970).

Chapter XI

MOSES BEFORE PHARAOH

After convincing his own people, the Hebrews, that he was indeed appointed by God to lead them out of Egypt, Moses went with Aaron before Ramses II, representing the God of the Hebrew people and, on God's behalf, requested that Pharaoh let the people go. Most of us are familiar with this portion of Scripture in which God, through Moses and Aaron, performs a series of miracles to convince the king of Egypt to let the Hebrew slaves leave, while the king refuses to do so after each miracle.

The consequences of Pharaoh's refusal to free the people were the ten plagues, recorded in the Bible, but totally absent from the Egyptian historical records. By this time, we should be used to the Egyptians' method of not recording anything that would detract from the authority and majesty of the king or of their gods. They did this, not just because they did not want to record "bad news," but mainly because of their belief in the magic of the spoken or written word. As previously noted, to speak or write about something was to give it life, existence. The reverse, to omit something or remove it, meant to deprive it of life, as if it had never existed. In the same manner, accounts could be embellished to the point of great exaggeration. To other cultures, this might seem to be outright lying. To the Egyptians, it was a way to make such accounts become reality.

An example of an embellished account in Egyptian history is the historic Battle of Qadesh, in which Ramses II is said to have been victorious over the Hittites. The truth about this battle was not learned until archaeological evidence showed that it was the Hittites who had won the battle; Ramses II had suffered a defeat.[167] However, this did not prevent the king from describing his success in glowing terms in an idealistic narrative. He also commissioned reliefs to be carved on the pylons of one of the major temples; in one pylon, Ramses II is shown in his chariot:

> "...charging bravely against the enemy, driving them back into the Orontes, beyond which stood the Hittite king, impotent, with his columns of uncommitted troops..."[168]

It is not surprising that events such as the plagues described in the Bible would not be mentioned in any records. Such plagues were the result of Pharaoh's disobedience to the God of the Hebrews and proof of the

---

167 T.G.H. James, op.cit., p.26.

168 K.A. Kitchen, op.cit., p. 64.

latter's superiority over the gods of Egypt. This is not the sort of information that the Egyptians wanted to leave for posterity.

However, a document exists that appears to support the premise that the plagues did occur. According to Immanuel Velikovsky, there was an eyewitness to the plagues—an Egyptian sage who wrote about events that are very similar to the Old Testament's description in Exodus. Velikovsky found in the translation of this document, the Papyrus Ipuwer,[169] several mentions of observable conditions such as, "The river is blood," and "Trees are destroyed...No fruit nor herbs are found." In Exodus, Moses had written, "All the waters that were in the river were turned to blood," and "...the hail smote every herb of the field, and broke every tree of the field." Moses wrote that "...there was a thick darkness in all the land of Egypt," and Ipuwer wrote, "The land is not light." The following chart with the Papyrus Ipuwer in the left column and the Exodus account of the plagues in the right column, highlights the similarities between the two.

Chart 8
Comparison of Two Descriptions of the Plagues

169 Immanuel Velikovsky, *Ages In Chaos*, (Garden City, N.Y.: Doubleday and Co., Inc., 1952), Vol. I, p. 40.

Alice I. Henry

*On the left is Papyrus Ipuwer and
on the right is the Exodus account*

	All the waters of the river
The river is blood	were turned to blood
	- Exodus 7:20
	The Egyptians dug around
Men... thirst after water	the river for water to drink
	- Exodus 7:24
Gates, columns, and walls are	And fire came down to earth
consumed by fire	-Exodus 9:23
Everywhere barley has	And the flax and the barley
perished	were smitten - Exodus 9:31
	The hand of the Lord is... on
The cattle moan because of	the cattle, which is in the
the state of the land	field - Exodus 9:3
	At midnight the Lord smote
	all the firstborn in the land
Men are few, and he who	of Egypt, from the firstborn
places his brother in the	of Pharaoh...to the firstborn
earth is everywhere	of the captive who was in
	prison - Exodus 12:29
The children of princes are	
dashed against the walls	
	I have sent forth my hand
	and smitten you and your
Pestilence is throughout	people with pestilence
	- Exodus 9:15

The land [was not light or bright]—this is a guess by translators. It is blank on the papyrus.	There was thick darkness in the land of Egypt - Exodus 10:22
Hair [has fallen out] for everybody	He whose hair has fallen out - Leviticus 13:40
Gold, lapis, silver...are strung on the necks	And they asked of the maidservants of silver and gold... and they plundered Egypt - Exodus12:35

The Papyrus Ipuwer resides in the Dutch National Museum of Antiquities in Leiden, Netherlands, but, unfortunately, the first third of the document is lost. There are certain parts of the papyrus that consist of fragments. The translator, A.H. Gardiner, has sections in his book[170] that are left blank, which, of course, makes it hard to understand what Ipuwer wrote or to place it in context with the rest of the document.

There have been many interpretations of the Papyrus Ipuwer—some say that Ipuwer had written a poem, speaking in prophecy about events that had not yet

---

170 Alan H. Gardiner, *The Admonitions of an Egyptian Sage*, Reprografischer Nachdruck der Ausgabe Leipzig 1909 Mit Genehmigung des Verlages J. C. Hinrichs, Leipzig. Georg Olms Verlag Hildesheim (1969). (Germany Herstellung: fotokop WiihelmWeihert, Darmstadt Best.-Nr. 5102 129) pp. 25-31

happened, while others say he was an eyewitness to cat-astrophic events, which could have been the plagues mentioned in the Bible. Some have tried to synchronize the biblical account with Ipuwer's papyrus, while others have had dissenting views about the Egyptian historical timeline versus the biblical timeline.

I have mentioned the Papyrus Ipuwer here, not as evidence of the plagues that fell upon Egypt—rather as "food for thought." I find it interesting that this papyrus appears to be the only account written by an Egyptian that alludes to a time of devastation experienced in Egypt—in the palace as well as throughout the land.

Let us return now to the biblical account of the plagues brought upon Egypt by the God of the Hebrews, through Moses and Aaron. There are several details worth discussing: One, the use of a rod by Moses and Aaron, as well as by the Egyptian magicians. In those days, a staff was carried by men of rank and was considered a badge of honor. Each stick was given a particular name and had its own significance. Its length was equal to a man's height; it was smooth, with a knob at the top; it was used as a walking stick and as a support for men when standing. The rod was a symbol of command or authority. In Egypt, it was thought of as a scepter of the gods.[171] The priests and magicians carried a rod as a special wand of office.[172]

---

171 A. Erman, op. cit., pp. 228, 229.

172 J.E. Manchip White, op. cit., p.46.

God used the rod carried by Moses and Aaron for the purpose of speaking to the Egyptians in their symbolic language. They clearly understood the significance of a rod. It was also used to speak to the Hebrews, who had been so immersed in the Egyptian culture and religion for so many generations that the message of the rod was made clear to them as well. They understood that Moses and Aaron were the official representatives of God, under whose power and authority they would speak and perform deeds.

Magic had not always been as central to Egyptian life in the palace as it was in the time of Ramses II. Magic gradually began to gain in importance as the word of the king decreased in its effectiveness. Circumstances, such as the Hyksos's domination and the Amarna heresy, under Akhenaton, contributed to changes in Pharaoh's manner of ruling the people. Haremhab counteracted the lessened respect for the power and authority of Pharaoh by enacting harsh laws, "impersonally by the state rather than personally by the pharaoh."[173] Under Seti I, magic and symbol began to take on more of an active role in administering affairs of state.[174] Since respect for the king's power and authority had continued to diminish, even strict laws could no longer be upheld without resorting to the use of magic.

---

173 J.A.Wilson, op. cit., p. 242.

174 M. Lurker, op. cit., p.7.

"The decrees of Seti I show another interesting factor, the invocation of magic to support law... It was no longer possible for pharaoh to issue his word, awfully potent because his divinity was unquestioned. Now he had to invoke the other gods by a curse to support his authority. The fear which had been his alone now had to be backed by magic. This later period...showed an increased reliance upon various magical techniques and powers. Insecurity brought a longing for greater protection through some kind of external potency. Men turned to magic scrolls and images of prophylactic power; they went through elaborate rituals when they recited charms. They tried to counteract the new fatalistic cast of life by summoning the gods for magical support. Man was no longer strong in himself."[175]

The God of the Hebrews spoke to Egyptians and Hebrews alike in the language of magic and symbol, with which they were so familiar.

Backing up a few steps in our discussion, we see another illustration of the great impact that his Egyptian upbringing had brought upon Moses: the importance of knowing a god's name. When being commissioned by God to deliver His people from slavery, Moses asked God what His name was to convince the Hebrew people that

---

175 J.A.Wilson, op. cit., p. 243.

he indeed was acting on God's behalf. God replied by revealing His name, "I Am." That is the name of God manifesting His eternal self-existence and almighty power.

Moses was to answer Pharaoh's question about God's name as well. What was the significance of knowing a god's name? James Breasted answers our question: It was the Egyptian belief that, "To know the name of a god is to be able to control him."[176] We can learn the basis for the importance of knowing a god's name from an account about Isis and Re, both Egyptian gods.

> "She (Isis) knew all things in heaven and earth as well as Re himself, but there was one thing which she did not know—and this want of knowledge impaired her power—the secret name of Re. For this god 'of the many names' kept his special name secret, the name on which his power was founded, the name which bestowed magical might on those who knew it... Then Re could no longer withstand the torment; he told Isis his name and regained his health through her magic power. Nevertheless, even after he was healed, the strong rule of the old sun-god had lost its vigour, and even mankind became hostile against him; they became angry and began a rebellion."[177]

176 J. Breasted, op. cit., p.107.

177 A. Erman, op. cit., pp. 265-267.

Although this story is a mythological account depicting gods with very human attributes, the God of Moses knew that the Hebrews and the Egyptians needed to believe that Moses and Aaron carried His own power and authority. And, through each of the plagues, God proved that He did not lose any of His own power and authority; on the contrary, He showed them that He was more powerful than their gods were.

God had told Moses that He would perform miraculous signs and wonders through him to prove to Pharaoh that He was God. Preceding the first plague, Pharaoh said that he did not know the God of the Hebrews and demanded to know who He was who commanded that the king of Egypt should obey Him.[178] When Pharaoh demanded to see a supernatural sign, Aaron was to throw down his staff before Pharaoh and it would become a snake. This is exactly what happened. Then, the king "summoned wise men and sorcerers, and the Egyptian magicians also did the same things by their secret arts: each one threw down his staff and it became a snake. But Aaron's staff swallowed up their staffs."[179] The Egyptians would not have been impressed at all by the turning of a rod into a snake; the Egyptian magicians had no hesitation about their ability to do the same with their rods.

"The turning of a serpent into what is apparently

---

178 Exodus 5:2.

179 Exodus 7: 9-12.

an inanimate, wooden stick, and the turning of the stick back into a writhing snake, are feats which have been performed in the East from the most ancient period; and the power to control and direct the movements of such venomous reptiles was one of the things of which the Egyptian was most proud, and in which he was most skillful, already in the time when the pyramids were being built...like the sage Abaner and king Nectanebus, and all other magicians of Egypt from time immemorial, he (Moses) and Aaron possessed a wonderful rod by means of which they worked their wonders."[180]

Another source states:

"When Aaron performed his wonder at the court, the king summoned his magicians, who were able to duplicate it. The text says that they did it 'with their spells,' which means that the trick was a standard item in their professional repertoire. Egyptian scarabs, those engraved ceramic or stone amulets or ornaments having the shape of a beetle, depict the magician performing the feat of holding a snake that is as stiff as a rod. This trick is reproduced in Egypt to this day by native snake charmers, and has often been described and photographed. The secret has been

180 E.A.Wallis Budge, op.cit., p. 5.

---

revealed as depending on the particular species of Egyptian cobra known as the "najehaje." Its distinctive feature is that it can be rendered totally immobile and absolutely rigid through the skilled application of great pressure to one of the nerves at the nape of the neck. When it is thrown to the ground, the jolt causes it to recover and the snake wriggles away."[181]

Although the magicians were able to imitate turning the rods into snakes, they were unable to imitate the second part, in which Aaron's rod swallowed their snakes, because this was not a magician's trick; rather, it was a supernatural act which God performed through Aaron. What was so significant about what Aaron had done versus the deed of the Egyptian magicians? Externally, there was nothing special about the feat. However, symbolically, God was conveying a message to the King of Egypt, and this did not go unnoticed. The Egyptians knew very well how to interpret symbolism in their religion:

"Religious ritual is not just a series of actions performed for their own sake. These acts are symbolic; that is, they refer to things other than themselves, and this reference is always to something in the world of the gods."[182]

181 Nahum M. Sarna, *Exploring Exodus, The Heritage Of Biblical Israel*, 2nd ed. (1986; rpt. New York: Schocken Books, Inc., 1987), pp. 67,68.

182 R.T. Rundle Clark, *Myth and Symbol In Ancient Egypt*, rev.ed. (1959;

God had, through Aaron, spoken to the Egyptians in the symbolic language of their religion, and they had understood the meaning. The message had to do with the significance of the snake to the Egyptian religion. The king wore an "uraeus," the goddess Buto, in the image of a rearing cobra with inflated hood, on his crown; this was a symbol of kingship and it was supposed to avert all evil.[183]

What God was saying was that, like the rod that swallowed the snakes of the magicians, He would overcome the goddess who protected the king and his kingdom from all evil. In other words, the message was that Pharaoh would be defeated by the God of the Hebrews. We might recall that the Egyptians believed that if they lost in battle, it simply meant the gods of the enemy were mightier than their own and therefore had overcome them. Through the following signs and wonders, the God of the Hebrews would judge and overcome[184] each of the Egyptian gods, thus proving His own superiority. This is not to say that God believed in the existence of the Egyptian gods; rather, that He was using a "symbolic language" that the Egyptians would not have difficulty understanding. Also, God's warnings preceding each plague were meant to show that His mercy and grace would

New York: Thames and Hudson, 1978), p.27.

183 Manfred Lurker, op.cit., p. 125.

184 Exodus 12:12.

intervene at any time, if Pharaoh became willing to obey Him and let the Hebrews go free.

In the next demonstration of God's power, God told Moses and Aaron, "Go to Pharaoh in the morning as he goes out to the water. Wait on the bank of the Nile to meet him..."[185]

This is historically accurate; every day Pharaoh did go down to the Nile River to engage in ritual washings:

> "Pharaoh's rising every day was a sacred occasion known as the 'Rite of the House of the Morning.' The king was first laved with water brought from the sacred lake which was part of the ritual equipment of each temple and palace. The water symbolizing the primordial waters of Nun, caused the king to be 'born anew.' He was then anointed, robed and invested with the royal insignia by two priests wearing the masks of Thoth and Horus."[186]

The god of the Nile, especially of the inundation, was called Hapi, who was also associated with Nun; he was:

> "...the father of the gods, for he was the sustainer and lord of the gods of the earth, of fertility and of creation."[187]

---

185 Exodus 7:15.

186 J.E. Manchip White, op.cit., p.41.

187 V. Ions, op.cit, p. 109.

Hapi's or Nun's primordial waters were used in the ritual which the king attended each morning. This is where Pharaoh had been when Moses and Aaron met him, at God's instruction. How ironic that the first plague zeroed in on "the father of the gods." Aaron was to stretch his rod over the Nile and all the canals, streams, ponds and reservoirs—even the water in wooden buckets and stone jars[188]—and the water would turn to blood. The Egyptians considered blood to be an abomination:

> "The Egyptians...regarded the Nile as a sacred stream, and worshipped it as a deity, calling it 'the Father of life,' and 'the Father of the gods.' The Egyptians, especially the priests, were very particular in their external habits and there was nothing which they held in greater abhorrence than blood, seldom admitting any bloody sacrifices. Their horror must therefore have been extreme when they found the river, which they worshipped as a god, turned into blood, which they regarded with such utter disgust."[189]

The fish died and the Egyptians could not drink the water—what an insult it was for the "father of life" to be the cause of death! What the God of the Hebrews was telling Pharaoh and the rest of Egypt, through the

---

188 Exodus 7:19.

189 Rev. James M. Freeman, A.M., *Manners and Customs of the Bible*, 2nd ed., (n.d.; rpt. Plainfield, New Jersey: Logos International, 1972), p.64.

symbolism involved, was that He judged their god of the Nile to be an abomination to Him, just as the blood was to them. He was saying that, instead of being the "father of life," their god caused death and that God Himself had defeated what they considered to be the "father of the gods." The Egyptians also believed that, not only was the conquering god superior to the defeated one, but the conquering god assimilated all the functions, attributes and characteristics of the conquered god.[190] In other words, they understood that the God of the Hebrews was the father or giver of life, that He was above any of their gods and that the Nile god they worshipped would only bring them death.

The Bible tells us that the magicians imitated what the God of the Hebrews had done through his representatives. Why would the Egyptian magicians imitate what happened through Aaron? Why would they desire to turn the Nile into blood? First, we are assuming that the magicians were able to cause such a change by their sorceries. They had a very elaborate system of magical formulae and rituals; some of the deeds they performed were no different from those done by our present-day magicians—done through trickery. In fact, we saw that they were able to change their rods into snakes just as Aaron had done, and we learned that this was a popular trick performed in those days.

---

190 V. Ions, op. cit., p. 1.

The reason the Egyptian magicians imitated the deeds God performed through Aaron is that they believed in homeopathy, treating like with like, and thus they were engaged in imitative magic. By duplicating God's deeds, the magicians were trying to neutralize their power.

> "Selket...was chiefly noted for her control of magic and, in particular, for treating scorpion stings by means of magic. It may seem strange that a goddess whose emblem was a scorpion should be concerned with nullifying its actions, but homeopathy—the countering of like by like—played an important part in ancient magic; no doubt she was believed to have at her command the particular poison contained in the sting of a scorpion and could use it for therapeutic purposes. Professional magicians are often mentioned in Egyptian texts as being attached in a priestly capacity to the cult of Selket..."[191]

Imitative magic was very much a part of the symbolic deeds done by the Egyptian magicians. Another example of this is the wooden figure of Tutankhamun found in his tomb:

> "By having this model in his tomb, Tutankhamun, through the process of imitative magic, would have an instrument that would enable him to be

191 I.E.S. Edwards, *Treasures of Tutankhamun*, (New York: Ballantine Books, a division of Random House, 1978), p. 155

reborn as the sun god every day."[192]

The Egyptian magicians were only able to imitate the first two plagues; after the third one, the plague of gnats, they said, "This is the finger of God."[193]

As each day God issued a warning if Pharaoh disobeyed, and each day Pharaoh's heart was hardened and he did not let the Hebrews go, God carried out His judgment of the Egyptian gods, through each successive plague.[194] Chart 9 shows the attributes of specific gods and the plague which might have judged them. Some of the Egyptian gods had more than one attribute and some shared similar attributes, perhaps because the Egyptians had many gods.

Chart 9

Plagues	Possible Egyptian Deities Attacked / Judged[195]
	Hapi: god of the Nile
1. Water Turned To Blood	Isis: goddess of the Nile
	Khnum: guardian of the Nile

---

192 I.E.S. Edwards, op. cit., p. 32.

193 Exodus 8:19.

194 Numbers 33:4.

195 Charles Swindoll, *Moses, God's Man For A Crisis*, 3rd ed. (1976; rpt. Fullerton, California: Insight For Living, 1985), pp. 56, 57.

2. Frogs	Heqet: goddess of birth, with a frog head
3. Gnats (or Mosquitoes)	Set: god of the desert
	Re: sun god
4. Insects (or Flies)	Uatchit: a god possibly represented by the fly
	Hathor: goddess with a cow head
5. Livestock Epidemic	Apis: the bull god, symbol of fertility
	Sekhmet: goddess with power over disease
6. Boils	Sunu: the pestilence god
	Isis: goddess of healing
	Nut: a sky goddess
7. Hailstorm	Osiris: god of crops, fertility
	Set: god of storms
	Seth: protector of crops
8. Locusts	Nut, Osiris, Seth: as above
9. Darkness	Re, Aten, Atum, Horus: all sun gods
	Nut, Hathor: sky goddesses
	Min: god of reproduction
	Isis: goddess protecting children
10. Death of the Firstborns	Heqet: goddess of birth
	Pharaoh (a god): his firstborn son

The tenth plague was devastating to everyone in the land of Egypt, except to those who followed God's instructions to avoid the death of the firstborn by putting the blood of the first "Passover" lamb on the doorposts and lintel of their houses.

The Bible tells us that the effect of this plague was felt everywhere in Egypt. It was felt even in the palace, where:

> "...from the firstborn of Pharaoh, who sat on the throne, to the firstborn of the prisoner, who was in the dungeon, and the firstborn of all the livestock as well," were struck by death.[196]

Since, through our research, we have ascertained that Ramses II was the pharaoh on the throne at this time, it follows that this plague must have killed his firstborn son. Certainly, such an important fact must be recorded in the historical records. Ramses II's firstborn son would be the next in line to the throne of Egypt—the son groomed from his early years to succeed his father. However, as is typical of Egyptian historians, there is no mention of a plague having caused the death of Ramses II's firstborn son. Nevertheless, evidence of the accuracy of the Bible is found indirectly, hidden, as it were, between the lines.

The historical accounts tell us that Ramses II's successor to the throne of Egypt was his son, Merneptah. Without further explanation and little emphasis, some

196 Exodus 12:29, 30.

of these accounts mention that Merneptah was Ramses's thirteenth son:

> "As the years passed the sons of his youth were taken from him and Khamwese was no longer there to conduct the celebration of the old king's jubilees. One by one they passed away until twelve were gone, and the thirteenth was the eldest and heir to the throne."[197]

One of Ramses II's firstborn sons, and heir to the throne, born to his favorite wife and sister, Nefertari, died when he was young; perhaps his death occurred on that fateful night when death touched most Egyptian households:

> "Nefertari's eldest son, Amun-her-khepeshef, appointed heir apparent by Ramses, was to be the first of many sons who predeceased their long-lived father. He died as a boy and was buried in a tomb near his mother's in the Valley of the Queens."[198]

We are not told how Ramses II's twelve sons died; nor do we know exactly when they died. Did their death occur at once, in one night—the night of the tenth plague? Or did their deaths happen over a period of years? However one might look at this, whether the death of the firstborn struck the palace and all at once twelve sons died,

---

197 J. Breasted, op. cit., p. 462.

198 L.K. Sabbahy, op. cit., p. 11.

or whether they died at different times, the fact remains that Ramses II's twelve dead sons had all been in the line of succession to the throne.

Remember that through marriage in the palace, Ramses's various queens, heiresses in the succession to the throne, bore him contenders to the succession. Some of these queens may have had more than one son. However, the very first consideration in the succession rested with Ramses's Chief Royal Consort or Great Royal Wife, Nefertari. When her firstborn son died, then the firstborn son of the second wife, Istnofret, Ramesses would have been the next heir. Following his death, the second born son of Nefertari, Amen-hir-khopshef, was next in line. After his death, the second son of Istnofret, Khaemwaset, was the next heir to the succession. As will be seen on Chart 10, Nefertari had eight more sons who died, one after the other, leaving Istnofret's third born son, Merneptah, Ramses II's thirteenth son, to ascend the throne after his father's death.

There are lists which mention Ramses II's children, one of which"...enumerates, although mutilated at the end, one hundred and eleven sons, while of his daughters we know of fifty-five."[199] Yet, none of the one hundred and eleven sons were even contenders to the throne.

K.A. Kitchen has researched these names and gives us a clearer picture of the sons who preceded Merenptah.

---

199 G. Maspero, op. cit., p. 243.

Chart 10 combines Maspero's and Kitchen's studies; it shows the names of sons of Ramses II and their order of birth, as well as the name of the mother of each. They are listed in birth order as fathered by Ramses II.

Chart 10
List of Ramses II's Wives and Heirs

NEFERTARI	ISTNOFRET	BINT-ANATH
1. Amen-hir-womef	2. Ramesses	Only had a daughter
3. Amen-hir-khop-shef	4. Khaemwaset	
5. Montu-hir-khop-shef		
6. Pre-hir-wonmef		
7. Sethy		
8. Meryre		
9. Meryre the Elder		
10, 11, 12, 14, 15. (There are five un-named sons between the above listed and the following, who was the sixteenth son)[200]	13. Merenptah (Ramesses II's 13th son)	
16. Mery-Atum		
17. Set-hir-khopshef		

---

200 K.A. Kitchen, op. cit., p. 102.

All the above-mentioned sons died before Ramses II's death, except for Merneptah, the thirteenth son, who became the next pharaoh. As seen on the preceding chart, Nefertari had twelve sons, who were born before Merneptah; and, according to K.A. Kitchen, every one of them met with death; the last four probably did as well. The succession then passed from her sons to the third son of Istnofret, Merneptah, who was the eldest surviving heir and who became the next king of Egypt, albeit in his sixties. He had not been trained as a crown prince. Ramses II could never have expected to lose twelve sons once they had passed the early childhood dangers that took the lives of young children in those days. He could never have expected that his thirteenth son would become heir to the throne.

One must wonder if Ramses thought back to the tenth plague that came upon Egypt on the night that led him to finally allow the Hebrews to go. Firstborn sons died throughout the kingdom on that first Passover in the households where parents did not obey God's command, through Moses—failing to mark the doorposts and lintel with the blood of the sacrificed lamb. However horrible that night might have been for those who lost their eldest sons, it was far worse for Ramses II, who lost not one crown prince, but twelve. Three of his crown princes died before Khaemwaset, Istnofret's second son, became the heir to the throne.

Granted, this did not all happen on that first Passover night. Nevertheless, it was even worse for Ramses because this plague continued to take his heirs to the throne over a period of several years. His fourth eldest son in the line of succession was a favorite, Khaemwaset. Five years after the tenth plague swept over Egypt, he, too, died. One by one, his crown princes died.

Such events cannot be ascribed to coincidence because the likelihood, the odds, were just too great to imagine; coincidence would be rendered impossible. Out of the one hundred and eleven sons that Ramses II is said to have had, can we assume that all firstborn sons of all his queens and concubines also died, most likely on the night of the tenth plague? Unfortunately, we will never know the full answer to this question—whether the other wives and concubines also lost their firstborn sons—as no details of their lives exist. However, the facts that we do have are sufficient to show us that, of all fathers in Egypt, Ramses II suffered the greatest losses.

We cannot imagine the anguish felt throughout the land of Egypt on the night of the tenth plague. The Bible describes it in these words:

> "And Pharaoh rose up in the night, he, and all his servants, and all the Egyptians; and there was a great cry in Egypt; for there was not a house where there was not one dead. And he called for Moses and Aaron by night, and said, 'Rise up,

and get you forth from among my people, both
you and the children of Israel; and go, serve the
Lord, as you have said.'"

The Hebrews received final instructions from God
about the observance of the Passover, which would com-
memorate how God delivered His people from slavery in
Egypt. Following that first Passover, the Bible says that
six hundred thousand men, not counting women and
children, as well as a great number who were a "mixed
multitude," left Egypt.[201]

Who were these people called a "mixed multitude?"
Obviously, they were non-Hebrews; perhaps they were
slaves from other countries; perhaps some were Egyptians
who had come to believe in the God of the Hebrews and
therefore decided to leave Egypt and her gods behind them.

It was not long before Ramses realized what he had
done in letting so many slaves, his main workforce, leave
Egypt. To rectify his error, he decided to pursue them with
his whole army in order to capture them and bring them
back. As he and the army followed the Hebrews, they
must have been filled with astonishment when they saw
the Hebrews cross the Red Sea. We are probably all familiar with the Bible's account about the miraculous parting
of the Red Sea so that God's people could cross it on dry
ground. However, when the Egyptian chariots followed
them into the Red Sea, the waters came down over them:

201 Exodus 12:34-51.

"And the waters returned, and covered the chariots, and the horsemen, and all the host of Egypt
that came into the sea after them; there remained
not so much as one of them."[202]

We might be tempted to assume that the Bible tells us
Pharaoh was included among those who died by drowning, since "there remained not so much as one of them."
That would mean that Ramses II would have drowned in
the Red Sea according to our previous conclusions. The
historical records all agree that Ramses II lived to be an
old man of ninety-two years; his mummy survives to this
day in the Cairo Museum, in exemplary condition and
no one has ever speculated that his death came about by
drowning. Besides this, the Exodus probably took place
in 1248 B.C., as mentioned earlier, accounting for the
forty years of wandering in the wilderness. Another fact
we've already mentioned is that by the time of the Israel
Stela (1208 BC), Israel is described as a free nation. Ramses
II was about fifty-six years old at the time of the Hebrews'
exodus, and we know that he lived another thirty-six
years, until his death in 1213 BC.

Therefore, it cannot be said that Ramses II drowned in
the Red Sea. Does this discredit our theories thus far? On
the contrary, it substantiates them. An understanding of
the Egyptian army's array for battle is necessary, at this
point:

---

202 Exodus 14:28.

"In a field of Action, it was the chariotry which took the first shock of battle, the infantry advancing behind them to exploit a tactical success or stem the enemy's advance if matters went awry. The chariotry also charged the enemy at the moment of victory, so as to turn a defeat into a rout, and it is doubtless this phase that we see those familiar pictures where pharaoh charges in his chariot over a carpet of dead and dying. There was also a 'corps d'elite' of infantry, known as the 'Braves of the King' or simply 'Braves.' It was their duty to lead the attack."[203]

It is clear from this information that the king of Egypt waited until victory was assured before plunging into battle. We can assume that the same tactic was used in going into the Red Sea. Besides this, the Bible states, "...and all the host (army) of Pharaoh that came into the sea..." denoting that not everyone in the army of Pharaoh "came into the sea." Pharaoh's position was at the end of the line of chariots,[204] waiting for his troops to present him with the signs of victory, usually:

"...a written account of the number of right hands and other limbs cut from the dead enemy on the battle field."[205]

203 L. Cottrell, op. cit., p. 114.

204 P. Montet, op. cit., p. 235.

205 J. Champollion, op. cit., p. 30.

In this case, Ramses II would have waited for a report about the Hebrews having been captured and brought back. Obviously, when Pharaoh saw the waters come down upon his army, he did not follow them; instead, he must have returned to the palace, defeated by the God of the Hebrews.

Although we can only speculate about the actual details following the Hebrews' crossing of the Red Sea, we do know that the king would not have drowned because, according to the usual array of the army, he simply would not have followed his men into the sea.

Chapter XII

Ramses II's Successor

The Egyptian historical records do not tell us anything that would make their pharaoh appear defeated neither by men nor by gods—especially a pharaoh as great as Ramses II. The best way to avoid having to tell about such events would be to skip the entire chapter describing life in Egypt when the Hebrew people lived in their land as slaves—this is exactly what they did; there is no such chapter. Yet, history does record the progressive decline of the Egyptian Empire after Ramses II's reign. Something must have occurred during the latter's reign that left the country in the hands of a weak and incapable old man as his successor was.

No allusion is made to a specific cause for such decline. However, we do know that death removed more capable contenders to the Egyptian throne. As we have discovered, the time and cause of their deaths is not mentioned. Who can say if their survival would have made a difference? We only know that the one who was never intended to rule, Merneptah—thirteenth in the line of succession—became the next pharaoh of Egypt. Could this have been the direct result of the tenth plague brought on by the God of the Hebrews?

The devastation Ramses suffered as the result of the tenth plague was felt by his dynasty after his death. Having ruled Egypt for sixty-seven years, he died at the age of ninety-two, leaving the throne to his aged son and successor. Whether due to Merneptah's advanced age by the time he became Pharaoh or to a weakness in his character, his rule led to the decline of the Ramessid Dynasty.

We might recall that God foretold this to Ramses II when, through Moses and Aaron, He supernaturally caused their rod-turned-to-serpent to swallow up the rods of the magicians, which had also turned to serpents through their magic tricks. As mentioned in the previous chapter, the message conveyed in symbols by this demonstration was that the king's power and authority over his kingdom would come to an end.

Although several years went by before this came to pass, not only did the Ramessid Dynasty become weakened and decayed after Ramses's death—it also ended abruptly only twenty-six years later. This is a very brief period when compared with the preceding more than two thousand years of continued grandeur in Egypt. With the end of the XIX Dynasty, Egypt has never recuperated its former splendor, the culmination of which had been reached under Ramses II.

Alice I. Henry

Was God harsh or unjust for allowing such a fate to befall Ramses and his kingdom? Considering the many opportunities which Ramses was given to believe in the superior power of the God of the Hebrews and to simply let His people go free, one would have to be very stubborn to cling to the opinion that Ramses and Egypt were undeserving victims. Had Pharaoh obeyed God right at the start, much suffering and death would have been avoided.

God *never* brought judgment upon Egypt without ample verbal and miraculous warning, prior to the demonstration of His power to carry it out—nor before giving the people an opportunity to have a change of mind and avoid judgment. Although God proved time after time that He meant what He said, Pharaoh chose to become more hardened and more obstinate, refusing to give in to the God of the Hebrews. We can say that Ramses brought the plagues upon himself and upon Egypt by his stubborn pride in refusing to free God's people.

Chapter XIII

The Case Against Coincidence in the Bible

Part One

We have arrived at the final chapters to be examined here. Thus far, we have concentrated our research on determining if what the Bible says about Moses can be substantiated by the Egyptian historical records. Whereas there seems to be a "Moses gap" in these accounts, we have attempted to show that the historical events and the biblical narrative are closely interwoven when we read "between the lines" and provide related facts. Apart from this, consider the time element: How easy would it be to pinpoint the exact time these events coincided in Egyptian and biblical history timelines?

Out of the more than three thousand years of Egypt's history, there is no other time when the biblical account of the Hebrew people and Moses could conform more precisely to the events in Egypt than the time of the New Kingdom, specifically the end of the XVIII and the beginning of the XIX Dynasties. We should remember that there are multiple people and events that we have attempted to chronicle.

We cannot give credit to chance at any time. We saw how the Hebrews entered Egypt because of Jacob's son, Joseph, being sold into slavery there. We saw how God guided the series of events that put him in a governing position second only to the pharaoh's office. We saw how a foreign, Semitic group of people ruled Egypt at a specific time in history. These Asiatic people, the Hyksos, were favorably disposed toward the Hebrews, also a Semitic people.

There is no coincidence found in the fact that documentation exists about only one pharaoh who, because of preceding historical events, found it necessary to rule with severity, issuing harsh edicts in an attempt to restore the throne of Egypt to its former position of respect and power. It would not be out of character for such a man to have considered the great number of Hebrew slaves as a threat to Egypt's safety and to have issued the edict demanding the death of every male Hebrew baby.

The coincidence is even less when we consider the specific time in Egyptian history when this pharaoh, Haremhab, came into power, in relation to the birth of Moses and the issuing of such an edict; it could not have been in effect three years before, when Aaron was born. When Moses was three months old, he was hidden in a basket placed in the river to keep him from being murdered.

The element of chance is further reduced when we realize that no other woman would fit the biblical description of "Pharaoh's daughter" as does Mutnodjmet, Pharaoh Ay's daughter who became Pharaoh Haremhab's wife. And remember that she was the only heiress to the throne of Egypt at that specific time; all other heiresses had died by then.

We can add to this growing amount of information that defies chance the fact that Mutnodjmet's mummy has been preserved and scientifically studied. Data from X-rays and CT-scans of Mutnodjmet showed evidence of multiple births. We know these were either stillbirths or deaths which occurred shortly after births, since we know that Haremhab had no heirs. This loss and grief would justify Mutnodjmet having secretly rescued and adopted the male Hebrew baby, Moses, as her own son to be raised in the palace as the next heir to the throne.

The time element features prominently in the argument against the randomness of chance. We can see this further illustrated by the fact that Moses fled from Egypt at the age of forty. At that exact time, the crown prince, who would have followed Seti I to the throne, disappeared from Egypt's records, leaving gouges on reliefs and carvings, and fading paint where his name or image were replaced by the one who had never been "crown prince," and therefore had never been intended to be the next king: Ramses II.

The Egyptians believed so strongly in the power of the spoken and written word that they thought they could change historical events by retelling, rewriting, or ignoring them. If they did not speak the name "Moses," the once Crown Prince who killed an Egyptian and escaped from Egypt, running for his life—then he became nonexistent in their minds. If they gouged hieroglyphs and reliefs with his name and his image, then Moses was never there. If Ramses II had his image and his name inserted in places where his "elder brother," Moses, had been, then this alteration of history is what the Egyptians fervently believed had happened.

Moses's return to Egypt forty years after his exile, his appearance, his speech, the signs and wonders God performed through him and Aaron, the plagues as judgments on the gods of Egypt—all of these can be clearly understood in the light of Egyptian religion, customs, and laws at this particular time.

It is as if the biblical view and the historical view, when studied apart from each other, are incomplete, leaving many unanswered questions that have led numerous people to discount the accuracy of the Bible. However, when these two views are interwoven, they support the accuracy of the Bible and make the Egyptian historical accounts clear and complete, filling in all the details they so painstakingly omitted in their attempt to present only those things that made them look good for posterity.

No—it wasn't coincidence that dictated these specific people and events coming together at a precise time in Egyptian history. The details presented by the Bible were not the result of human planning; rather, they came about through the meticulous organization of a higher mind than man's—the Bible tells us that it was God, through His knowledge of past, present, and future, who orchestrated the events and the specific people to come together in a definite place and time—in Egypt in the XVIII and XIX Dynasties.

To make the case for divine planning more convincing than coincidence, we can turn to the laws of probability. Fortunately, there is a book in which the author simplifies the concept of probability by citing some prophecies found in the Old Testament of the Bible and showing the chance of their fulfillment in the New Testament. He does this to illustrate how "...coincidence is ruled out by the science of probability."[206]

Part Two

We have looked at the events in the life of Moses and the Hebrew people he led out of slavery in Egypt. Reading between the lines that were written about this period of Egyptian history and looking at its mirror image shown

206 Josh McDowell, *Evidence That Demands A Verdict*, Vol. I, rev.ed., (1972; rpt. San Bernardino, CA: Here'sLifePublishers,1979), p. 167.

170

in the Bible, we can say that the Bible is accurate in every detail surrounding the life of Moses and the Hebrews in Egypt. God had told Abraham that his descendants would become slaves and that their deliverance would take place four hundred and thirty years later "to the day." This was the length of time that God had foretold, which occurred exactly on the fifteenth day of Nissan (our March/April), the day of the first Passover observance. Therefore, it must also be possible to prove the accuracy of the rest of what the Bible says, from the first page to the last.

This proof can be found in the fulfillment of the Old Testament prophecies, not only literally in the time they were written, but also in a future time, in the New Testament. After all, in those days, one of the ways to prove if a prophet was real or not was whether his prophecies came true or not. If they did not, then the punishment was that the prophet would be stoned to death. One may wonder why anyone would have wanted to accept such a responsibility; yet all the prophets in the Bible accepted it, even in the face of a death sentence if they were not believed. They preferred being put to death by men rather than being disobedient to God.

There are many good books written about the Bible and prophecy. I especially like two volumes written by Josh McDowell entitled *Evidence that Demands a Verdict*. In speaking about the fulfillment of Old Testament prophecies in the New Testament, he uses the laws of probability.

Some may argue that there are coincidences in how some of the prophecies were said to be fulfilled. However, McDowell disproves this by giving several examples. In one of these, he quoted Peter Stoner, Professor Emeritus of Science at Westmont College:

> "'Coincidence is ruled out by the science of probability.' Stoner has computed the probability of Jesus Christ fulfilling eight prophecies written about Him hundreds of years before. In his research, Peter Stoner took the following eight prophecies:
>
> 1. Born at Bethlehem (Micah 5:2; Matthew 2:1)
>
> 2. Preceded by a Messenger (Isaiah 40:3; Matthew 3:1-3)
>
> 3. He Was to Enter Jerusalem on a Donkey (Zechariah 9:9; Luke 19:35-37)
>
> 4. Betrayed by a Friend (Psalm 41:9; Matthew 10:4)
>
> 5. Sold for Thirty Pieces of Silver (Zechariah 11:12; Matthew 26:15)
>
> 6. Money to Be Thrown in God's House and Price Given for Potter's Field (Zechariah 11:13; Matthew 27:5, 7)
>
> 7. Dumb Before Accusers (Isaiah 53:7; Matthew 27:12)

8. Hands and Feet Pierced (Psalm 22:16; Luke 23:33)

(In Roman crucifixion, hands and feet were pierced by large, dull spikes) and Crucified with Thieves (Isaiah 53:12; Matthew 27:38).'"

"Stoner states:

'We find that the chance that any man might have lived down to the present time and fulfilled all eight prophecies is 1 in 10 to the 17th power (or 1 chance in 100,000,000,000,000,000...(If) we take 10 to the seventeenth power silver dollars and lay them on the face of Texas...they will cover all of the state two feet deep. Now mark one of these silver dollars and stir the whole mass thoroughly, all over the state. Blindfold a man and tell him that he can travel as far as he wishes, but he must pick up one silver dollar and say that this is the right one. What chance would he have of getting the right one? Just the same chance that the prophets would have had of writing these eight prophecies and having them all come true in any one man, from their day to the present time, providing they wrote them in their own wisdom...the fulfillment of these eight prophecies alone proves that God inspired the writing of those prophecies to a definiteness which lacks only one chance in 10 to the seven-teenth power of being absolute.'"[207]

This is only one example. There were many more prophecies that were fulfilled in the New Testament. During Jesus Christ's life on Earth, three hundred and thirty-two prophecies about Him were fulfilled by Him.[208] It's mind-boggling to think of how many zeroes would follow the probability that so many prophecies could be fulfilled by one man in a specific manner in just over thirty years when he walked on Earth. These things were attested to by eye-witness accounts written by the four evangelists and by Peter and Paul. The latter saw the res-urrected Christ while on the road to Damascus, where he was headed to give the order to put Christians to death. He was converted and became a follower of Christ after his miraculous encounter.[209]

Apart from the Bible, *Antiquities of the Jews*, written by the Jewish historian Flavius Josephus and published in 93 or 94 A.D., recorded the resurrection of Christ as a historical event:

> "Now, there was about this time, Jesus, a wise man, if it be lawful to call him a man, for he was a doer of wonderful works—a teacher of such men as receive the truth with pleasure. He drew

207 J. McDowell, Inc.,op.cit. p. 270.

208 Josh McDowell, op.cit. p. 175.

209 Acts 9: 6 -20

over to him both many of the Jews, and many of the Gentiles. He was [the] Christ; and when Pilate, at the suggestion of the principal men amongst us, had condemned him to the cross, those that loved him at the first did not forsake him, for he appeared to them alive again the third day, as the divine prophets had foretold these and ten thousand other wonderful things concerning him; and the tribe of Christians, so named from him, are not extinct at this day."[210]

In the fifty-third chapter of the Book of Isaiah, the prophet, who lived about seven hundred years before Christ, there is a detailed description about the death of Jesus Christ and the events surrounding the crucifixion:

"Surely he took up our pain and bore our suffering,yet we considered him punished by God, stricken by him, and afflicted. 5 But he was pierced for our transgressions, he was crushed for our iniquities; the punishment that brought us peace was on him, and by his wounds we are healed.

6 We all, like sheep, have gone astray, each of us has turned to our own way; and the LORD has laid on him the iniquity of us all.

---

210 Flavius Josephus, *The Complete Works of Josephus*, trans. William Whiston, A.M., rev.ed. (1960; rpt.Grand Rapids: KregelPublications, 1981), p. 379.

7 He was oppressed and afflicted, yet he did not open his mouth; he was led like a lamb to the slaughter, and as a sheep before its shearers is silent, so he did not open his mouth."[211]

Through inspiration, God gave these and other prophecies to different Old Testament authors, spanning a period of over one thousand five hundred years. The proof that the Old Testament prophets were real and spoke God's message is in the fulfillment of the prophecies revealed in the New Testament.

Some may say that the Old Testament was not finished about four hundred years before the birth of Christ. They might say that it was written after major life events of Jesus Christ had already happened; others may say that, since there have been so many translations, we can expect mistakes to have been made. However, these arguments—or excuses to doubt the accuracy of the Bible—can be refuted by evidence that these writings, which comprised the entire Old Testament, were finalized at least two hundred and fifty years before the birth of Christ.

At that time, there was a translation of the Old Testament books of the prophets from the Hebrew language to Greek. It is known that the scribes who copied the Old Testament or Torah—the Hebrew law, which comprised the first five books of Moses, and the prophets—did it painstakingly. If a scribe made even a tiny

---

grammatical error in copying the text, he would tear up the entire page or scroll where he found the mistake, and start again from the beginning, always checking and re-checking meticulously.

The reason for the Greek translation can be understood in the following quotation from Josh McDowell's book:

> "All of the Old Testament prophets were translated into Greek in the Greek Septuagint by about 280-250 BC. Therefore, we can assume that all of the prophets (including Joel and Obadiah) were written before this time.
>
> In order to have the need of a translation, we would have to assume that the original language in which the Old Testament was written was not Greek (in fact, it was Hebrew) and therefore was older than the translation. In a letter, written by a court official of King Ptolemy to his brother around 250 BC, we can find evidence about this translation. The official refers to six elders chosen by the Jewish high priest who were sent to Alexandria, along with an especially accurate copy of the Torah, which they translated in seventy-two days, (the 'Septuagint')presenting an agreed version as the result of conference and comparison."[212]

---

212 J. McDowell, op. cit., pp.58, 59.

Based on the above examples, we can say that the Old Testament prophets were genuine because their prophecies, given to them by God, were perfectly fulfilled at just the right time.

Considering the authenticity of the prophets and prophecies in the Old Testament, we might ask what God's purpose might have been in using people to speak for Him. What was His main message, spoken through the prophets—specifically, through the man Moses?

Chapter XIV

THE GOD OF THE HEBREWS AND HIS MESSAGE

Thus far, I have used the Christian Bible when referring to Moses, his birth and life in Egypt, and later in Midian; his role in speaking to Pharaoh about the impending plagues if God's people, the Hebrews, were not allowed to leave Egypt; his role in the Exodus as leader of a multitude's forty-year sojourn in the wilderness. I write from my perspective as a Christian, using the Christian Bible as the reference. However, we can also find the same story of Moses told in the Hebrew Torah—the first five books of the Law, written by Moses, as taught in Judaism. The Tanakh, another Jewish name for the entire Hebrew Scriptures, consists of twenty-four books, including the Torah and all the same books that are in the Bible's Old Testament. Moses is also considered to be the most important prophet in Islam and in many other religions that trace their descent to Abraham.

What was the message that the God of the Hebrews wanted to announce to His people?

"But the Tanach (*Tanakh*) is much more than

just history. In it one can learn about G-d's plan for the world and of His relationship with mankind..."[213]

It would be nice if we could say that, having been delivered from slavery, the Hebrews lived happily ever after. However, as our human nature frequently shows us, none of us is perfect. Stubbornness can keep us from receiving all the blessings God has in store for us, just as it kept the Hebrews from arriving at the land—"flowing with milk and honey"—the Promised Land. Despite God's demonstration of His power in delivering them from slavery, when things went well, they faltered in their trust in Him and turned away from Him.

Whenever the people rebelled against God, He allowed neighboring peoples to attack them. When their affliction became unbearable, they turned back to God and cried out for His help. Every time they returned to God in repentance (turning away from their own will to God's), He forgave them and blessed them. They repeated this back-and-forth behavior over and over, during all their years of wandering in the desert of the Sinai Peninsula. Yet, despite their wavering trust in God, He forgave them every time they repented and returned to Him.

Throughout Psalm 106, we can read about this repeated scenario:

"Many times He delivered them; but they

---

rebelled in their counsel, and were brought low for their iniquity. Nevertheless He regarded their affliction, when He heard their cry; and for their sake He remembered His covenant, and relented according to the multitude of His mercies."[214]

Having witnessed the power of their God in delivering them out of over four hundred years of slavery in Egypt, having seen the miracles that God performed through his servants Moses and Aaron, one would think that they would have had enormous faith in God: that He would work things out and that they would be alright in His care, that they would make it through the wilderness because God was with them. He had miraculously fed them and given them water to drink in the desert; He had supernaturally kept their clothes and shoes from wearing out despite all the wandering they did during the forty years, as it says in the Old Testament:

"Your garments did not wear out on you, nor did your foot swell these forty years."[215]

Yet, throughout the wandering of the Hebrew people in the desert of Sinai, we see them struggling with their faith in their God, and in His human representative, Moses.

Even Aaron, Moses's own brother, had his faith

---

214 Psalm 106:43-45

215 Deuteronomy 8:4

shaken when Moses, who had climbed Mt. Sinai to speak with God, failed to return in a timely fashion. Aaron even imagined that Moses had died on the mountain, so he assumed the leadership of the Hebrews. Even worse than doubting that Moses would return to continue to lead them, Aaron doubted in the God who had shown Himself to possess all power.

Instead, Aaron had a golden calf built out of the gold that some of the people in Egypt had given to them as they left for the Red Sea. Aaron and the Hebrews prayed to the golden calf they had made with their own hands, asking for it to lead them. In doing this, they reverted to the Egyptian god Apis and made an idol of it for them. All the people joined right in, chanting and dancing in their worship of the golden calf. Before Moses returned from Mt. Sinai carrying the tablets of stone containing the Ten Commandments written by God's own finger, the people had already disobeyed every one of them. And, even so, when they repented, God forgave them.

God's laws (commandments) were not meant to teach them, or us, obedience. Rather, they were meant to show the disobedience inherent in mankind's human nature, as they tried to obey its rules and regulations and saw that they could not abide by them in their own efforts. God's laws are like a mirror whose image shows what we're really like apart from God's will. The Commandments were given so that the people then, and we now, might repent of our own ways of trying to please God; and that we might seek God's deliverance from the slavery to sin, which is defined as rebellion against God's will in favor of our own will. The events in Exodus show clearly that only God could have provided that deliverance—both then and now.

The Book of Exodus illustrates how the generation that was delivered from slavery in Egypt and that wandered around, literally in the circles of their own stubborn heart, died in the wilderness. The generation that was born in the wilderness after them—the generation who believed in the promise, led by Joshua—made it out of the desert and to the Promised Land.

Again, it would be wishful thinking to say that the new generation found the proverbial happy ending. Throughout the centuries, God's people continued to waver in their faith, according to how good or bad their circumstances were. For that reason, God continued to send prophets over that time span, speaking God's words: calling for repentance, calling for a turning away from their own ways and the world's ways, toward God's way, which He ultimately provided in the flesh in the New Testament.

In the Old Testament, God showed Moses that He required specific, though temporary sacrifices that would foreshadow their total fulfillment, once and for all, through the Lamb of God, on the altar of the cross at Mt. Calvary. It was the lamb sacrificed in each household on that first Passover, whose blood was sprinkled on the doorposts and lintels, which would enable their firstborn to survive the tenth plague, death.

That was Moses's mission—to tell the people God's message. God always spoke His message in ways the people could understand. He used sacrificial animals and rituals as symbols to convey the central message: He wanted the people to have a relationship with Him, and that God Himself was the one to give the instructions as to how to obtain this relationship through faith in Him--the only One who could provide the atonement.

From the very beginning, in Genesis, the first book in the Old Testament, God provided the sacrifice to restore the broken relationship that Adam and Eve's sin brought about—their disobedience and rebellion against God's will. It was the literal animal (I imagine it very likely to have been a lamb) that God provided for Adam to sacrifice that symbolically restored his and Eve's relationship with God, although the consequence of their disobedience had changed the nature of the relationship. They had to leave the Garden of Eden and could no longer see God face to face.

There were many consequences that came with Adam and Eve having chosen to disobey God—the first one was separation from Him. Nevertheless, God provided the sacrifice to restore the broken relationship. Genesis tells us that an innocent victim shed its blood to cover their sin: Another consequence was that they could no longer live in the presence of God on Earth. They had to leave Eden and experience all the hardships that living in this world would entail. And, eventually, after more than nine hundred years, they would die physically. Yet, they believed—through faith in God because of their restored relationship with Him through His provision of a sacrifice—that after death, they would live forever in the presence of God in Heaven—in "paradise," which means "the presence of God."

This is the message that Moses spoke to the people who left Egypt with him—the blood of the sacrificed lamb had to be put on every doorpost and lintel so that, when the last plague came, the angel of death would "pass over" them. And this is the same message that the prophets preached in the Old Testament—the message that was finally fulfilled in the New Testament by God's innocent, sacrificial victim, the true "Lamb of God," Jesus Christ. This is the message of the Gospel—salvation from eternal death—the "good news."

Epilogue

O ur journey has now come to its end. Have we found
   the answers to the questions we had at its beginning? Was Moses a real person who was just as the Bible
portrays him? Did the exodus of the freed Hebrew slaves
actually take place? Did the Hebrews really wander in the
wilderness for forty years? I believe that the evidence presented thus far, found between the lines of history when
compared to the Bible, proves these and other aspects in
the life of Moses to be true.

There was only one place in the timeline of Egyptian
history when the biblical events surrounding Moses and
God's people, the Hebrews, could have taken place—the
period between the end of the XVIII Dynasty and the beginning of the XIX Dynasty. There were only certain definite
historical Egyptian figures that could have fit as precisely
as they did into the Bible's account of the life of Moses.

The Bible specifically mentioned "Pharaoh's daughter" and we found that Mutnodjmet was the daughter
of Pharaoh Ay; she was the only surviving heiress who
could provide a claim to the throne for her father's successor, Haremhab, through his marriage to her.

Haremhab, the one known for his harsh edicts, could well have issued the orders to put to death all male Hebrew babies. The impact of this edict would have significantly reduced the Hebrew population, which, at that time, was far greater than the Egyptian population. His intention was to prevent Egyptians from suffering another foreign takeover, as happened in the time of the Hyksos invasion from Asia.

Haremhab appointed his successor, Ramses I, to be the next pharaoh who reigned until his untimely death about two years later. His son became Pharaoh Seti I, a contemporary of Moses.

In Chapter VII, we found evidence of a crown prince who was not Seti I's successor to the throne. This crown prince would have been raised and trained in the palace to become the next king of Egypt. However, this mysterious figure disappeared suddenly and was never again mentioned. At about the same time, Seti's ten-year old son, Ramses, who had never held the title of Crown Prince, began to feature in carvings and paintings as the heir to the throne. Nevertheless, time has revealed that a different crown prince had been painted underneath the later peeling paint. Carvings of this unknown crown prince had been gouged out and supplanted by the figure and names of Ramses II.

After Seti I's death, Ramses II became Pharaoh. His monumental building projects required a large slave population to provide the labor. When the exodus of the Hebrews occurred, Ramses II was in his fifties. During this specific period, the Bible tells us that the Egyptian task masters put so many demands on the slaves that the latter became ready to listen to God's message through Moses; this resulted in the Exodus. This event occurred on a specific day, "four hundred and thirty years to the day," as God had foretold to Abraham. We learned that the precise day the Exodus occurred was the fifteenth day of the Hebrew month Nissan (our March/April), because this was the date of the very first Passover as recorded in the Hebrew texts and in the Bible. The Israel Stela confirmed this further by leading us to the year 1248 BC as the year of the Exodus.

We discovered that Pharaohs Ay, Haremhab, Seti I, and Ramses II and Mutnodjmet, daughter of Pharaoh Ay and wife of Haremhab were the only people in Moses's "cast of characters" whose roles and periods in which they ruled could fit the biblical narrative for the events in the life of Moses.

In the fifth year of the reign of Merneptah, son of Ramses II, we found confirmation that the freed Hebrews were referred to as "Israel" in the Israel Stela, which had carved words describing Israel battling against the Libyans. This is the first time that Israel is mentioned, showing that by 1248 BC, God's people were no longer slaves, but a nation fighting to conquer other lands.

When the historical and biblical facts are intertwined, the Moses gap is filled. The Bible is the key that decodes the enigma of the missing Moses in Egyptian history.

If we believe that God is a Higher Being who knows more than we do, and who can inspire people over the course of fifteen hundred years to write the sixty-six books that make up the Bible, we must conclude that the message within those pages is important. Just concentrating on a single book of the Bible, we might ask ourselves: *Why would the message in the Book of Exodus be important to the many generations that have come and gone since the events mentioned on those pages occurred? Could it be that the message still applies today, as it did to all the previous eras in history?*

I believe that God can write a message within a message, one that was literally fulfilled in the time of Moses, yet also one that has applied to all succeeding generations, including our own. This message within a message, or the spiritual truth behind the story of Moses in the Book of Exodus, might not only be about the Hebrews, but about all fallen mankind throughout the ages who, like the Hebrews, have tried and are still trying to find a way out on their own, not trusting in God.

So...what could that message be? To the Hebrew slaves, it was a message of deliverance from the years of slavery, a promise of being guided to a better place, the land "flowing with milk and honey"—the comfort of knowing that God would be with them and bless them.

If they believed in and turned to and relied on Him, He would meet all their needs on their journey through life. How would that apply to our time?

It still is a message of deliverance, which is a synonym for the word "salvation." God's message to our time, as in all preceding times, is one of salvation through believing and trusting in Him, turning to Him, relying on Him to guide us through our journey in life on this earth. All the Old Testament prophecies pointed to the day when God Himself would come to Earth in the person of Jesus Christ, to die on the cross at Calvary—to take our place and pay the price for our sin—our rebellion, our separation from God, our following our own will instead of His—just as the Hebrews did throughout their time in the wilderness. He wants to be our Passover Lamb and to deliver us from eternal death—separation from Him.

God fulfilled all the prophecies in the Old Testament, and He will continue to fulfill His promises until the end of time. We saw in "Chapter XIII—The Case Against Coincidence in the Bible"—convincing statistics on the laws of probability—how God could perfectly fulfill just a few of the prophecies that were foretold through the prophets by His inspiration.

We can picture ourselves as slaves to the idols, the things and ways of this world that are in opposition to His will. The choice is ours: Turn to Him in repentance, which means turning one hundred and eighty degrees from our way to His way. He has provided the sacrificial death of an innocent, sinless victim, the true Lamb of God, Jesus Christ, God in the flesh. What He did on that cross, He did personally for each individual human being on Earth. Sadly, not all are willing to accept His salvation—His free, unmerited gift (the definition of "grace")—but prefer to continue in their own way, wandering in the circles, in the wilderness of their own heart.

Why have I invited you to join me on this journey to find the historical Moses? Because, if this man could historically be proven to have existed, just as the Bible says, if he really did live in Egypt and was raised in the palace to be Crown Prince and future Pharaoh, if he walked among and interacted with historical figures at a particular time and place in Egypt—then the message found in the rest of the Bible should warrant serious thought.

I picture a mathematical equation: If what the Bible says about Moses can be proven in every detail—thus eliminating the historical Moses gap that the Egyptian writings, paintings, carvings, and documents have been shown to have—then the rest of the message in the Bible must be true as well. We might then need to ponder just how important that message must be!

Acknowledgements

Iwould like to thank Mary Lib Morgan, my editor at Perfectly Penned. It was delightful to work with her. Many thanks to Stephanie Fowler and Andrew Heller at Salt Water Media for putting what once were just thoughts inspired by research and typed on pages, a published reality. I am grateful to Lynn McLain, an attorney whose expertise in discussing copy right law, as it applied to the various sources I used in the book, was most helpful. To Cynthia Rae Lauer, my friend of many decades who put the desire in me to explore the Bible—so many thanks! And a very big thank you to my husband, Michael, our sons Guy and Oliver, and our daughter Jennifer, for their love and encouragement...and patience.

Bibliography

Aldred, Cyril, *Akhenaten King of Egypt.* London: Thames and Hudson Ltd., 1991.

Aldred, Cyril. *Akhenaten and Nefertiti.* New York: The Viking Press, Inc., 1973.

Anker, Charlotte, Danforth, Kenneth C., Somerville, Robert, eds. *Lost Civilizations-Egypt: Land of the Pharaohs.* Alexandria, Virginia: Time-Life Books, 1992.

Breasted, James Henry. *A History of Egypt.* New York: Charles Scribner's Sons, 1937.

British Museum. London: Egyptian Hall, Room 65, wall painting reproduction, "Sethos I Charging the Lybians, Karnak."

Budge, E.A. Wallis. *The Dwellers on The Nile.* New York: Dover Publications, Inc., 1997.

Budge, E. A. Wallis. *Egyptian Magic.* New York: Dover Publications, Inc., 1971.

Champollion, Jacques. *The World of The Egyptians.* Geneva: Minerva, 1971

Clark, R. T. Rundle. *Myth and Symbol in Ancient Egypt.* New York: Thames and Hudson, 1978.

Cottrell, Leonard. *Life Under The Pharaohs.* New York: Holt, Rineheart and Winston, 1960.

David, Ph.D., Rosalie A. *The Making of the Past—The Egyptian Kingdoms.* Oxford, England: Phaidon Press Ltd., 1975.

DeHaan II, Martin R. *Knowing God Through Exodus.* Grand Rapids: Thomas Nelson, Inc., Publishers, 1989.

Desroches-Noublecourt, Christianne. *Life and Death of a Pharaoh, Tutankhamen.* New York: Little, Brown and Company, 1978.

Duffield, Guy P. *Handbook of Bible Lands.* Glendale, California: Regal Division G/L/Publications, 1971.

Edwards, I.E.S. *Treasures of Tutankhamun.* New York: Ballantine Books, a division of Random House, 1978.

Encyclopaedia Britannica. Chicago: William Benton, Publisher, 1961.

Erman, Adolf. *Life in Ancient Egypt.* New York: Dover Publications, 1971.

Freed, Rita E. *Ramses II, The Great Pharaoh and His Time.* Denver: Denver Museum of Natural History, n.d.

Freeman, A. M., Rev. James M. *Manners and Customs of the Bible.* Plainfield, New Jersey: Logos International, 1972.

"Herp" Magazine. "Reptiles and Amphibians of the Bible Lands" by Roy Pinney. Bulletin of the New York Herpetological Society, Vol. XI, No. 1 and 2, December, 1974.

Hobson, Christine. *The World of the Pharaohs*. Thames and Hudson, 1987.

Hutchinson, Warner A. *Ancient Egypt, Three Thousand Years of Splendor*. New York: Grosset& Dunlap, 1978

Ions, Veronica. *Egyptian Mythology*. London: Hamlyn, 1968.

James, T.G.H. *Pharaoh's People*. Chicago: University of Chicago Press, 1984.

Keller, Werner. *The Bible As History*. New York: William Morrow and Company, 1980.

Kitchen, K.A. P*haraoh Triumphant, The Life and Times of Ramesses II, King of Egypt*. Warminster, England: Aris & Phillips Ltd., 1985.

Lurker, Manfred. *The Gods and Symbols of Ancient Egypt*. London: Thames and Hudson Ltd., 1984.

MacQuitty, Wm. *Tutankhamun, The Last Journey*. New York: Crown Mc Publishers, 1978.

McDowell, Josh. *Evidence That Demands a Verdict*, Vol. I. San Bernardino, CA: Here's Life Publishers, 1979.

Maspero, G. *History of Egypt*. Vol. V of XIII. London: The Grolier Society Publishers, 1903. A. H. Sayce, Editor. McClure Translator.

Montet, Pierre. *Everyday Life In Egypt, In the Days of Ramesses The Great.* Trans. A.R.Maxwell-Hyslop and Margaret S. Drower. Philadelphia: University of Pennsylvania Press, 1981.

Morsley, H.V. *Junior Bible Archaeology.* New York: Roy Publishers, Inc., 1963.

Murray, Margaret Alice. *The Splendor That Was Egypt.* New York: Hawthorn Books, Inc., Publishers, rev. ed, 1963 (1949).

National Geographic. December, 1982, p. 762.

The NIV Study Bible. Michigan: The Zondervan Corporation, 1985.

Sameh, Waley-el-dine. *Daily Life in Ancient Egypt.* n.p.: "Short Records" Publisher, 1964.

Sabbahy, Lisa K. *Ramses II: The Pharaoh and His Time.* Provo, Utah: Brigham Young University Print Services, 1985.

Sarna, Nahum M. *Exploring Exodus, The Heritage of Biblical Israel.* New York: Schocken Books, Inc., 1987.

Sellman, R. R. *Ancient Egypt.* New York: Roy Publisher, 1960.

Stead, Miriam. *Egyptian Life.* Cambridge, Massachusetts: Harvard University Press, 1986.

Steindorff, George and Seele, Keith C. *When Egypt Ruled the East.* Chicago: The University of Chicago, 1957.

Swindoll, Charles. Moses, *God's Man for a Crisis.* Fullerton, California: Insight For Living, 1985.

White, J. E. Manchip. *Ancient Egypt, Its Culture and History.* New York: Dover Publications, Inc., 1970.

Wilson, John A. *The Burden of Egypt.* Chicago: University of Chicago Press, 1951.

Wilson, John A. *The Culture of Ancient Egypt.* Chicago: University of Chicago Press, 1963.

Velikovsky, Immanuel. *Ages in Chaos.* Garden City, New York: Doubleday and Co., Inc., 1952.

Vos, Howard F. *An Introduction to Bible Geography.* Chicago: Moody Press, 1983.

www.ingramcontent.com/pod-product-compliance
Lightning Source LLC
Chambersburg PA
CBHW030825090426
42737CB00009B/875